COMING TO
KNOW
CHRIST

COMING TO
KNOW
CHRIST

ROBERT L. MILLET

DESERET
BOOK

Salt Lake City, Utah

Library of Congress Cataloging-in-Publication Data
Millet, Robert L., author.
  Coming to know Christ / Robert L. Millet.
    pages cm.
  Includes bibliographical references and index.
  ISBN 978-1-60907-013-7 (hardbound : alk. paper)
1. Jesus Christ—Mormon interpretations. 2. The Church of Jesus Christ of Latter-day Saints—Doctrines. 3. Mormon Church—Doctrines. I. Title.
  BX8643.J4M545 2012
  232—dc23   2012003639

Printed in the United States of America
Publishers Printing, Salt Lake City, UT

10 9 8 7 6 5 4 3 2 1

CONTENTS

CONTENTS

Chapter 1
AFTER THE IMAGE
OF OUR OWN GOD

Simon Peter had spent three years beside his Master, traveling from village to village, gazing with awe as Jesus ministered to the widows, healed the children of Roman officials, taught the gospel of the kingdom, exposed and condemned the hypocrisy and self-righteousness of his enemies, and sought to prepare his chosen Twelve for his eventual departure. Peter had been privy to sacred and unspeakable moments, had witnessed firsthand the mercy and majesty of this most unusual and powerful man, this Jesus of Nazareth. He had, in private quarters, seen the dead brought back to life. He had, in the midst of multitudes, beheld the lowly Nazarene feed five thousand men, plus women and children, with only five loaves of bread and two fishes.

Simon had, on the holy Mount, been transfigured, lifted spiritually to a higher plane, with his Lord and his apostolic associates James and John; had heard the voice of God the

Father speak out of the Shekinah, the holy cloud; and had received the more sure word of prophecy and thereby gained the assurance of eternal life (2 Peter 1:19; D&C 131:5–6).[1] He had witnessed the arrest of Jesus, had beheld at least a part of the mock trials, and had seen his world come crashing down as the Messiah yielded himself to the hands of sinful men and the ignominy of death by crucifixion. Peter's was a cold, dark, and dreary world for three days, as the Jews counted time.

But the morning of resurrection came. Reports reached the senior apostle that the tomb was empty, that Christ had burst the bands of death, that Jesus had risen from the grave. Eventually Peter was blessed with a personal appearance of the risen Lord and also met with him in company with the other apostles on several occasions. Simon was delighted but mystified. Excited but confused. Thrilled but full of questions. What did it all mean? What were they to do, this tiny band of loyal apostles, to perpetuate the work of the Master when the Master was soon to leave them? Only these eleven souls could know the depth of anxiety and perplexity that must have surged through their hearts and challenged their minds as they witnessed the ascent of Jesus the Christ, their Savior and Redeemer, into the heavens.

"There were together" at the Sea of Galilee "Simon Peter, and Thomas called Didymus, and Nathanael of Cana in Galilee, and the [two] sons of Zebedee [James and John], and two other of his disciples. *Simon Peter saith unto them, I go a fishing.* They say unto him, We also go with thee" (John

21:2–3; italics added). Unclear of what they should do, uncertain of how their ministry should proceed, the apostles of the Lamb of God, those chosen to bear witness of the name of Christ in all the world (D&C 107:23), returned to their boats and their nets. It was business as usual. It would be some weeks before the Pentecostal outpouring would take place, some time yet before the testimony and grasp of the perspective and poignancy of the Resurrection would dawn upon them, the sure knowledge of it would be planted in their hearts by the power of the Holy Spirit, and they themselves transformed into bold and indefatigable witnesses of what had transpired and of how this gospel of the kingdom would indeed be spread throughout the known world.

On the same day that these brethren returned to their nets, still devoid of vision, and sat on the seashore and ate fish prepared by the resurrected Redeemer, "Jesus saith to Simon Peter, Simon, son of Jonas, lovest thou me *more than these?*" (John 21:15; italics added). Did He mean, Simon, son of Jonas, do you love me more than any of the other apostles love me? Or was it, Simon, son of Jonas, do you love me more than you love the other apostles? Or did He mean, Simon, son of Jonas, do you love me more than you love these fish? Or, Do you love me more than your old business, your old way of life? If so, then let's get back to *our* business; we have work to do. If you truly love me above and beyond all else, feed my lambs. Feed my sheep.

That scene, of course, is familiar to every Christian. We have heard scores of sermons and lessons on the importance of caring for others as a sign of our love for the Savior (compare Matthew 25:40; Mosiah 2:17). But how often have we taken the time and exercised the mental and spiritual energy to turn the terrible question upon ourselves? "Bob, do you love me more than these home furnishings, these stock portfolios, these elegant automobiles, these expensive toys? Do you love me more than position and prestige? Do you love me more than public esteem, social acclaim, or the flattery of prominent men and women? Are you more concerned with 'Christ esteem' than you are with self-esteem? Are you more wedded to my work and glory (Moses 1:39) than you are to your company's mission statement? Do you know what my will is for you? Does my will really matter more to you than your will does?"

Such questions get at the essence of having an eye single to the glory of God (D&C 88:67), of yielding our hearts to God (Helaman 3:35). They strike at the very core of who we are, why we are, what we do, what we refrain from doing, and what drives and directs our feelings, attitudes, and behaviors. They are the kinds of questions—haunting and penetrating as they are—that when pondered, reflected upon, and attended to regularly in earnestness and sincerity, mold our character and transform our human nature. They are a significant part of turning a natural man into a saint (Mosiah 3:19), an old sinner into a new creature in Christ (2 Corinthians 5:17; Mosiah 27:26).

In his best-selling book *The Purpose-Driven Life*, Pastor Rick Warren suggests that one of the first things our Heavenly

Father may choose to ask us at the judgment bar is simply this: "What have you done with my Son?"[2]

What a question! Is it not essentially the same as such questions as, Where does Jesus fit in your life? Is he the central feature, the divine center? Or is he ancillary, tangential, and at best an accessory to everything else in your daily walk and talk?

We must not allow Jesus Christ to become just another facet of our lives, any more than religion must be permitted to become one of many realms of our souls. "I can well understand," C. S. Lewis said, "how a man who is trying to love God and his neighbour should come to dislike the very word religion, a word, by the way, which hardly ever appears in the New Testament." Too many people, Lewis went on to say, "substitute religion for God—as if navigation were substitutes for arrival, or battle for victory, or wooing for marriage, or in general the means for the end. But even in this present life, there is danger in the very concept of religion. It carries the suggestion that this is one more department of life, an extra department added to the economic, the social, the intellectual, the recreational, and all the rest. But that whose claims are infinite can have no standing as a department. Either it is an illusion or else our whole life falls under it. We have no non-religious activities; only religious and irreligious."[3]

It would not be correct, either historically or theologically, to state that the light of divine direction went out and God's care and concern and even involvement with his children on earth ceased in A.D. 100 and did not reappear until the spring of A.D. 1820.[4] It would be appropriate, however, to speak of an apostasy following the deaths of Christ and the meridian apostles: a falling away in which apostolic priesthood authority was lost, plain and precious truths lost or corrupted, and persons during those centuries had "transgressed the laws, changed the ordinance, broken the everlasting covenant" (Isaiah 24:5). Where apostolic oversight is missing, spiritual mischief or even well-intentioned mistakes more readily crop up.

In the Preface to his book of Doctrine and Covenants, Jesus Christ spoke: "And the arm of the Lord shall be revealed; and the day cometh that they who will not hear the voice of the Lord, neither the voice of his servants, neither give heed to the words of the prophets and apostles, shall be cut off from among the people; for they have strayed from mine ordinances, and have broken mine everlasting covenant; they seek not the Lord to establish his righteousness"—and now note the divine *description* of modern idolatry—"but every man walketh in his own way, and after the image of his own god, whose image is in the likeness of the world, and whose substance is that of an idol, which waxeth old and shall perish in Babylon, even Babylon the great, which shall fall" (D&C 1:14–16).

There it is—the *description* of the world at the time of Joseph Smith. Idolatry in its many forms had spread its subtle influence among the people of the earth. But now note the Lord's *prescription* for the modern malady: "Wherefore, I the

Lord, knowing the calamity which should come upon the inhabitants of the earth, called upon my servant Joseph Smith, Jun., and spake unto him from heaven, and gave him commandments" (D&C 1:17). In short, the restoration of the fulness of the gospel came as a remedy, an aid, an elixir for toxic times, a solution to many of the problems facing a world that did not enjoy apostolic and prophetic direction, a world in which there were certainly foundational Christian teachings and values and virtues but a world in which heaven-sent doctrine and covenants and ordinances needed desperately to be put back on track.

The Restoration took place to reenthrone the true and living God, to bear witness of the corporeality of the Father of our spirits, in whose image each of us is created; of the resurrected Jesus Christ as our Lord and Redeemer, a separate personality and a distinct being from the Father, whose mission of mercy makes salvation or eternal life available to the penitent, and whose matchless example charts a course for how we should and must live among our brothers and sisters if we are to claim the title of Christian; and of the Holy Ghost as a spirit, the third member of the Godhead, the Witness, Testator, Comforter, and Sealer. The revelations of heaven came to us through the Prophet Joseph Smith so that we might know *what*, meaning *Whom*, we worship (D&C 93:19). Further, God's plan of salvation, his great plan of happiness, began to be unfolded so that the Saints of the Most High might understand what things matter most in this life, what things are worthy of our reflection and even our reverence. Seers, living oracles, have been called and put in place in order that the children of God might know to praise the praiseworthy, to turn away from the tawdry, to relish the righteous, and to shun the shoddy. In a world too prone to yield to the shifting sands of secularity and to follow the madding crowd to do evil, living prophets provide the certain sound of the trumpet (1 Corinthians 14:8), a warning against that which defiles and dilutes our discipleship, a herald of hope—hope for a better world here and hereafter—for those who center their faith and worship in God.

Rather than walking in their own way, true disciples walk in the path pointed out and prepared by their Master. Instead of creating God in their image, true Saints seek to be conformed to the image of Christ (Romans 8:29) and to allow that image to shine in their countenances (Alma 5:14). Instead of visiting Babylon frequently and eventually perishing there, true sons and daughters of God seek to build up Zion and establish the righteousness of the Righteous One on earth (JST, Matthew 6:33; JST, Luke 12:31). In short, people of the covenant are called upon to focus their attention and rivet their affection upon God and the things of God. To do otherwise is to yield to the spirit of idolatry and thereby to pursue a path that leads to disillusionment, doubt, and ultimately, destruction.

President Spencer W. Kimball explained: "Few men have ever knowingly and deliberately chosen to reject God and his blessings. Rather, we learn from the scriptures that *because the exercise of faith has always appeared to be more difficult than relying on things more immediately at hand, carnal man has tended to transfer his trust in God to material things.* Therefore, in all ages when men have fallen under the power of Satan and lost the faith, they have put in its place a hope in the 'arm of flesh' and in 'gods of silver, and gold, of brass, iron, wood, and stone, which see not, nor hear, nor know' (Daniel 5:23)—that is, in idols. . . . *Whatever thing a man sets his heart and his trust in most is his god;* and if his god doesn't also happen to be the true and living God of Israel, that man is laboring in idolatry."[5]

In a world like ours, in a time when men and women "wander from sea to sea, and from the north even to the east," when they "run to and fro to seek the word of the Lord" (Amos 8:12); when "many yet on the earth among all sects, parties, and denominations" are "blinded by the subtle craftiness of men, whereby they lie in wait to deceive," when such noble people "are only kept from the truth because they know not where to find it" (D&C 123:12)—in such a time as this, it is vital that we discover God, the "only true God, and Jesus Christ, whom [he has] sent" (John 17:3). It is vital that we learn the lesson of the ages, the lesson that whole civilizations either forgot or trampled under their feet—that peace and happiness in this life and glory and honor everlasting in the life to come are available only to those who divest themselves of worldly lusts and *presentism* and invest themselves in righteousness, holiness, and *eternalism*. "Where there is no vision, the people perish" (Proverbs 29:18). Where vision exists, including that elevated perspective provided only by the gospel of Jesus Christ, the people prosper and are preserved in safety.

"Why did God put the first commandment first?" President Ezra Taft Benson asked. "Because He knew that if we truly loved Him we would want to keep all of His other commandments. 'For this is the love of God,' says John, 'that we keep his commandments' (1 John 5:3; see also 2 John 1:6).

"We must put God in the forefront of everything else in our lives. He must come first, just as He declares in the first of His Ten Commandments: 'Thou shalt have no other gods before me' (Exodus 20:3).

"When we put God first, all other things fall into their proper place or drop out of our lives. Our love of the Lord will govern the claims for our affection, the demands on our time, the interests we pursue, and the order of our priorities.

"We should put God ahead of *everyone else* in our lives."[6]

Modern revelation expands this singular truth: "Thou shalt love the Lord thy God with all thy heart, with all thy might, mind, and strength; and in the name of Jesus Christ thou shalt serve him" (D&C 59:5). We need God. We must have God in our lives if we are to survive. Our souls should seek after God's living word and his liberating love. When the roadblocks and detours of a world gone astray have been cleared away, the path to our Heavenly Father, to his Beloved Son, and to life eternal with them and with our families, is open to us, and the way ahead is revealed by their marvelous light. We are on course.

Chapter 2
PEOPLE OUGHT TO KNOW

I have always believed there is a God. Among my earliest memories of childhood are the familiar words spoken beside my bed each night: "Now I lay me down to sleep . . ." It felt right to say my prayers, and I sincerely believed that I was being heard by someone far wiser, greater, and more powerful and loving than anyone here on earth. Further, having grown up in the southern states, with most of my friends being Baptists, Methodists, or Roman Catholics, I sang songs with them, such as "Jesus loves me, this I know, for the Bible tells me so" and "Jesus wants me for a sunbeam," with gusto and feeling. It seems that I have always believed in the living reality of Jesus Christ as the Savior and Redeemer of humankind.

My grandfather joined The Church of Jesus Christ of Latter-day Saints in the 1930s near New Orleans, Louisiana. He had been brought up as a Roman Catholic, and so when he left the faith of his fathers, he was basically asked to leave home as well. Later he and my grandmother raised their four sons as Latter-day Saints. By the time I was born, my father and mother were not active church attenders, but in time they felt the need to raise their children in the Church.

When I was about nine years old, I was asked to speak in a church meeting. My father did not feel at that early stage of his spiritual development that he was in a position to help me much, and so my uncle Joseph essentially wrote my talk for me. I memorized it. It was a very simple recitation of Joseph Smith's First Vision—the story of how young Joseph wrestled in 1820 with the question of which church to join, how he encountered varying and conflicting views on religious issues, and how he chose to follow the scriptural admonition to ask God for wisdom (James 1:5).

It has now been more than fifty years since I looked out at that rather frightening congregation, delivered those halting words (that talk couldn't have lasted more than four or five minutes), and then sat down with a feeling of overwhelming relief. I also remember something else about that occasion—namely, how I felt at the time I spoke about God the Father and his Son Jesus Christ appearing to a fourteen-year-old boy in upstate New York. Although I was, as one might expect, nervous and fidgety behind the pulpit, I began on that occasion to feel the stirrings of testimony, the beginnings of a spiritual witness that what I was speaking about was true and that it had actually happened. The relief I felt afterward was not simply the flood of emotion associated with having completed a daunting task but also the quiet yet poignant assurance that I had spoken the truth. I knew something when I sat down that I had not known as clearly when I stood up to speak.

I also have a clear recollection of my first awkward attempt to bear a testimony in public. I had through the years felt very deeply about God, about the Savior, and about the Church, but I had never borne testimony to my branch or ward members. I remember coming home from a fast meeting when I was a little over fifteen years of age. As I recall, my mother had been ill that day and had stayed home. As I was changing clothes I overheard a conversation between Mom and Dad, one that hurt a bit. Mom asked: "Did he bear his testimony today?" My dad, who was then the bishop of the ward, responded simply: "No, he just sat there with his forehead against the back of the bench in front of him."

Those were painful words for me, mostly because I wanted to please my parents and not in any way disappoint them. I felt the spirit of testimony within my bosom, but I just didn't feel the courage to stand up in front of so many people and speak freely of things that were deeply personal. Within a few months however, I managed to conjure up the courage during a pause in the testimony meeting and make my way to the stand. I started out fine and felt that expressing my testimony wouldn't be such a big deal after all.

But then feelings that were deep down, feelings I had had for a long, long time, came to the surface, and with them came emotions that were very powerful and very unexpected.

For some reason, my tear ducts and my mouth are linked, such that whenever I begin to feel emotion, I can't seem to form words properly. In short, I stood before that large body of people and cried. Not something a sixteen-year-old enjoys doing. I returned to my seat, promptly rested my forehead against the back of the bench in front of me, and waited anxiously for the meeting to be over. When amen was said, I raced out the doors and went and sat in the car. I felt ashamed. I felt embarrassed. I feared that I had somehow done an injustice to the ward and to myself, that I had borne a poor testimony.

Dad finally came home about four o'clock that afternoon. He walked down the hallway and stopped at my room. I was lying on my bed, still feeling pain from the meeting, when Dad stuck his head around the door, smiled, and said, "For what it's worth, I've never been more proud of you than I am right now." I tried to apologize for the way I had acted, but he would have none of it, assuring me that each of us is different and that bearing a testimony of sacred things affects everyone differently. "As long as your testimony is sincere," Dad said, "I think the Lord is happy with how you do it."

Thousands of times over the years I've heard someone stand and say, "I want to bear my testimony that I know the gospel is true." In my young life I had supposed that a testimony of the gospel was the same as a testimony of the Church, and so I assumed such individuals were merely expressing their witness of the importance of the Church in their lives. Many, many times I've heard people say, "I know *this gospel* is true." In all honesty, I have found myself on several occasions asking, What gospel is that? Is our gospel any different from anyone else's? Is it better? Is it more complete? Does ours have more stuff in it?

It really wasn't until I was back from a mission that I began to study carefully just what the gospel is. I learned in the scriptures (3 Nephi 27:13–14; D&C 76:40–42) that the gospel is the good news, or glad tidings, that Jesus Christ had come into the world to be our Savior and our Redeemer; that through our sins and misdeeds we had distanced ourselves from our Heavenly Father, had gotten off the straight path, and needed someone who was the Way to point the way back home; that if Jesus had not been born, had not taught the principles of salvation, had not suffered and bled and died and risen from the tomb—in other words, if Christ had not performed his singular mission, we would be left without hope.

The Prophet Joseph Smith was once asked what the fundamental principles of our religion are. If reporters from *Time, Newsweek, U.S. News & World Report,* or the *Washington Post* were to interview you and ask that very question, how would you respond? Would you say that the fundamental principles of our religion are the teachings found in the Word of Wisdom concerning the proper care of our physical body? The sealing powers associated with the eternal family unit? The knowledge that we lived before we were born and that we will live again after we die? That when the Lord Jesus referred to the many mansions of his Father, he had reference

15

to the kingdoms of glory hereafter? That temples are erected to link heaven and earth, time and eternity, past, present, and future? Indeed, what *are* the fundamental principles of our religion? All of these are important teachings, in fact, some of the distinctive features of Mormonism. Joseph Smith did not choose at that early date to mention any of these beliefs, although I am certain that he would today feel they are very important parts of our faith. Rather, he taught that the fundamental principles of our religion "are the testimony of the Apostles and Prophets, concerning Jesus Christ, that He died, was buried, and rose again the third day, and ascended into heaven; and all other things which pertain to our religion are only appendages to it."[1]

The New Shorter Oxford English Dictionary defines *appendage* as "something attached; a subsidiary adjunct; an addition; an accompaniment." Further, the word *subsidiary* means a supplement, an auxiliary, something subordinate or secondary.

Do we appreciate what the Prophet Joseph is teaching us here? He is trying to tell us that there is a truth, a central truth that is like the hub of a bicycle wheel; the spokes of the wheel are very important, but they are all connected to the hub.

In 1977, President Boyd K. Packer gave a remarkable address entitled "The Mediator," a very touching and instructive message on how it is only through Jesus that God's justice and mercy can be properly balanced and satisfied. "Truth, glorious truth, proclaims there is . . . a Mediator,"

President Packer testified. "Through Him mercy can be fully extended to each of us without offending the eternal law of justice." Now notice what President Packer had to say about this key doctrine: *"This truth is the very root of Christian doctrine.* You may know much about the gospel as it branches out from there, but if you only know the branches and those branches do not touch that root, if they have been cut free from that truth, *there will be no life nor substance nor redemption in them."*[2]

In other words, Christ is the Divine Center: his life and atoning sacrifice and resurrection give meaning and purpose to everything else we do. We pray to the Father in the name of the Son because Jesus is our Savior. We plead for forgiveness of our sins because Jesus is our Redeemer. We take the sacrament of the Lord's Supper each week because Jesus is our Paschal Lamb; he offered his broken body and spilt blood in sacrifice for you and me. Temples and eternal families have no meaning if we do not understand that they are not ends in themselves but rather means to a greater End, even the Master. Do we fully appreciate that truth? How about our friends of other faiths? Do they know just how central Jesus Christ is to everything we believe?

You and I are faced on all sides by people who insist we are not Christian and who are even bold to declare that Latter-day Saints worship a different Jesus than the Christ of the New Testament. You know better than that, and so do I. But sometimes our friends don't, and it just may be the case that they do not hear enough about our feelings for the Lord

Jesus Christ or our commitment to him and our testimony of him to convince them otherwise.

"Are we Christians? Of course we are!" President Gordon B. Hinckley stated. "No one can honestly deny that. We may be somewhat different from the traditional pattern of Christianity. But no one believes more literally in the redemption wrought by the Lord Jesus Christ. No one believes more fundamentally . . . that He rose from the grave, and that He is the living, resurrected Son of the living Father."[3]

Our faith must not be a secret. Nor must the central feature of our faith be kept under wraps. We need to let others know just how we feel about Jesus Christ and how vital to our own lives are his life and death. To say this all another way, some things simply matter more than others. Some topics of conversation, even intellectually stimulating ones, must take a back seat to more fundamental truths. It is just so in regard to what the scriptures call the gospel or the doctrine of Christ, those foundational truths associated with the person and powers of Jesus the Messiah. Who he is and what he has done are paramount and central issues; all else, however supplementary, is secondary.

Chapter 3

IF JESUS IS THE ANSWER, WHAT'S THE QUESTION?

Several years ago, while driving through Florida and Georgia, I noticed a number of billboards along the way with a fascinating message in large and bold print: "Jesus is the answer!"

I smiled and agreed. After I had driven a few more miles, still reflecting on the billboards, I wondered what Jews or Muslims or Buddhists or Hindus might think about such a message. I wondered if anyone might have asked, "Oh, really? Well, then, what's the question?"

Answers are always much more appreciated when we know what the questions are. What are some of the questions to which "Jesus Christ" is the most correct answer?

• *Where is peace to be found in this troubled day?*

We live in a world filled with noise, violence, and tons of distractions. Speaking for myself, one of the reasons it's harder than it should be to focus on Christ and the Atonement during the brief period of the sacrament on the Sabbath day is that I haven't learned sufficiently to discipline my mind and heart to block out lesser things so that I can attend to greater things.

Pain is all about us. Sorrow and abuse and heartbreak are around each corner. Wars and rumors of wars abound. Man's inhumanity to man and indifference to God are evident on the front page of the paper. Jesus and his servants, the prophets, surely knew that such times would come, that men's hearts would fail them, that love would wax cold, and that sweet affections would be twisted or distorted. He knew that our lives would be cluttered, filled with ten thousand times ten thousand things to do, and that we would be tempted, again and again, to be caught up in the thick of thin things.

Knowing all this, however, the prophets have been consistent: we must look to God and live (Alma 37:47).

We live in a telestial world today, one in which ugliness, deceit, indifference, and cynicism surround us. It would be too easy for us to give in, agree with the masses, and be led captive by voices that beckon to us to follow them into despair. But the apostles and prophets of our day have told us there's a better way, a clearer picture, a more abundant life to be found. Peace can come to us in this troubled world only through looking to the Lord Jesus Christ and yielding our hearts unto him (Helaman 3:35). Surrendering to the world will lead to slavery, while standing up for what we believe and looking to the divine Head of the Church for direction and answers will bring peace.

Some years ago President Boyd K. Packer issued a challenge to the young people of the Church. He stated that as a young person he "knew what agency was and knew how important it was to be individual and to be independent, to be free. I somehow knew there was one thing the Lord would never take from me, and that was my free agency. I would not surrender my agency to any being but to Him! I determined that I would *give* Him the one thing that He would never take—my agency. I decided, by myself, that from that time on I would do things His way.

"That was a great trial for me, for I thought I was giving away the most precious thing I possessed. I was not wise enough in my youth to know that because I exercised my agency and decided myself, *I was not losing it. It was strengthened!*"[1]

It's a difficult lesson to learn, but I bear personal testimony that what President Packer taught is right on target. The happiest days of my life have come when I have chosen to forgo what I wanted to do and instead do things the Lord's way. There's a quiet but real confidence that comes to us by the power of the Holy Spirit when we align our will with God's. That is the stuff from which spirituality is made; the spiritual person is the one who has gained the complete victory over self through being willing to make an unconditional surrender of self to a higher power.

In his Last Supper, the Savior offered the following

invitation and instruction: "Peace I leave with you, my peace I give unto you. . . . *Let not your heart be troubled, neither let it be afraid*" (John 14:27; italics added).

That injuction, Elder Jeffrey R. Holland observed, "may be one of the Savior's commandments that is, even in the hearts of otherwise faithful Latter-day Saints, almost universally disobeyed; and yet I wonder whether our resistance to this invitation could be any more grievous to the Lord's merciful heart.

"I can tell you this as a parent: as concerned as I would be if somewhere in their lives one of my children were seriously troubled or unhappy or disobedient, nevertheless I would be infinitely more devastated if I felt that at such a time that child could not trust me to help or thought his or her interest was unimportant to me or unsafe in my care.

"In that same spirit," Elder Holland continued, "I am convinced that none of us can appreciate how deeply it wounds the loving heart of the Savior of the world when He finds that His people do not feel confident in His care or secure in His hands or trust in His commandments.

"Just because God is God, just because Christ is Christ, they cannot do other than care for us and bless us and help us if we will but come unto them, approaching their throne of grace in meekness and lowliness of heart. They can't help but bless us. They have to. It is their nature."[2]

Think about what the following scriptures teach us:

"Be careful for nothing [don't be overly concerned about

anything]; but in every thing by prayer and supplication with thanksgiving let your requests be made known unto God.

"And the peace of God, which passeth all understanding, shall keep [guard] your hearts and minds through Christ Jesus" (Philippians 4:6–7).

"These things I have spoken unto you, that in me [Jesus] ye might have peace. In the world ye shall have tribulation: but be of good cheer; I have overcome the world" (John 16:33).

"Wherefore, fear not even unto death; for in this world your joy is not full, but in me your joy is full" (D&C 101:36).

Few hymns touch me as deeply as the following one:

> *Where can I turn for peace?*
> *Where is my solace*
> *When other sources cease to make me whole?*
> *When with a wounded heart, anger, or malice,*
> *I draw myself apart,*
> *Searching my soul?*
>
> *Where, when my aching grows,*
> *Where, when I languish,*
> *Where, in my need to know, where can I run?*
> *Where is the quiet hand to calm my anguish?*
> *Who, who can understand?*
> *He, only One.*
>
> *He answers privately,*
> *Reaches my reaching*

In my Gethsemane, Savior and Friend.
Gentle the peace he finds for my beseeching.
Constant he is and kind,
Love without end.[3]

• *Some of my friends seem to be changing their values and their standards. When I try to do as I've been taught, they call me goody-goody and say that I need to adapt to changing times. Is there anything constant in our world? Is there anything or anyone I can rely on with complete confidence?*

It takes a pretty strong person, a rather unusual young person, to stand up to ridicule and refuse to give in to temptation. There are so many things today in modern music, on television, and in the movies that portray a life that is nowhere near the life the Lord would have us live. Consequently, we cannot afford to turn to the radio, television, or Hollywood for our cues about what is right and what is wrong. It is scary to realize that the more we are exposed to Hollywood's version of life, the more we gradually begin to accept it.

Our world is becoming less and less bothered by the crude, the harsh, and the unkind. More and more often we see on the silver screen men and women who live together and raise children without marriage, families that are dysfunctional, families in which the father is an embarrassing and unnecessary buffoon, characters whose vulgar and profane language imply that such language is the norm.

Let's face the facts: The world may have its standard, but

Christ and his prophets have another standard altogether, a standard that those who are members of his Church are expected to maintain.

It wouldn't matter the snap of two fingers if the entire population of the world agreed that abortion is okay, that premarital sex is acceptable, or that drug abuse is just the way things are. God says otherwise! And so, when the winds and the waves of temptation attempt to storm our fortress of faith, we must look to the one constant, the one never-changing source of peace and perspective—Jesus Christ and the principles of his eternal gospel. The risen Lord declared to the Nephites: "Therefore, hold up your light that it may shine unto the world. *Behold I am the light which ye shall hold up*—that which ye have seen me do" (3 Nephi 18:24; italics added). In our dispensation that same Savior offers these consoling words: "Learn of me, and listen to my words; walk in the meekness of my spirit, and you shall have peace in me" (D&C 19:23).

• *I have watched painfully as my brother/sister/parent has chosen to leave the faith and go astray. He/she seems to have abandoned everything he/she was ever taught. Family members' and friends' pleadings seem to fall on deaf ears. Can anything be done? Is there anyone who can help?*

Almost always we speak of someone searching for the gospel and finding It. There are times, however, when the Lord does the searching, when he who has been called "the

Hound of Heaven" pursues the wanderer, touches and softens his hardened heart, and leads him back to the fold.[4]

We must never forget that one of our Lord's most beloved titles is that of the Good Shepherd. When a sheep goes astray in search of greener grass and more pleasant grazing, seldom does that sheep make its way back by finding the shepherd. Rather, the Good Shepherd, the one who knows and loves his flock, who knows them one by one, leaves the ninety and nine and goes on a search-and-rescue mission in behalf of the one. The Good Shepherd does not stop loving the wandering sheep, nor does he conclude, "Well, ninety-nine out of a hundred isn't bad. There's no use wasting time on one lousy sheep." Because the shepherd has in fact paid a price to raise his sheep, to feed and protect them, to lead them, and to know them well, he feels a great sense of responsibility to see to their care; he will not leave them out in the desert to wander forever.

Elder Orson F. Whitney offered the following powerful commentary: "The Prophet Joseph Smith declared—and he never taught more comforting doctrine—that the eternal sealings of faithful parents and the divine promises made to them for valiant service in the Cause of Truth, would save not only themselves, but likewise their posterity. Though some of the sheep may wander, the eye of the Shepherd is upon them, and sooner or later they will feel the tentacles of Divine Providence reaching out after them and drawing them back to the fold. *Either in this life or in the life to come, they will return.* They will have to pay their debt to justice;

they will suffer for their sins; and may tread a thorny path; but if it leads them at last, like the penitent Prodigal, to a loving and forgiving father's heart and home, the painful experience will not have been in vain. Pray for your careless and disobedient children; hold on to them with your faith. Hope on, trust on, till you see the salvation of God. . . .

"You parents of the wilful and the wayward! Don't give them up. Don't cast them off. *They are not utterly lost. The Shepherd will find his sheep.* They were his before they were yours—long before he entrusted them to your care; and you cannot begin to love them as he loves them. *They have but strayed in ignorance from the Path of Right, and God is merciful to ignorance.* Only the fulness of knowledge brings the fulness of accountability. Our Heavenly Father is far more merciful, infinitely more charitable, than even the best of his servants, and the Everlasting Gospel is mightier in power to save than our narrow finite minds can comprehend."[5]

In verses that we seldom sing but that are filled with the spirit of reaching out to the lost and struggling, we find the following soothing promise :

> *When through the deep waters I call thee to go,*
> *The rivers of sorrow shall not thee o'erflow,*
> *For I will be with thee, thy troubles to bless, . . .*
> *And sanctify to thee thy deepest distress.*
>
> . . . .
>
> *E'en down to old age, all my people shall prove*
> *My sov'reign, eternal, unchangeable love;*

And then, when gray hair shall their temples adorn, . . .
Like lambs shall they still in my bosom be borne.

The soul that on Jesus hath leaned for repose
I will not, I cannot, desert to his foes;
That soul, though all hell should endeavor to shake, . . .
I'll never, no never, no never forsake![6]

• *My mom/dad/sibling/friend just passed away. How am I going to make it? How can I face life without her/him? How can this horrible hole in my heart be filled?*

There is nothing more common to this life than death; it is the common lot of all who come into this life to leave it. Everyone is born, and everyone must die. We are all born as helpless infants, and we all depart this sphere equally helpless in the face of death. Even among those who read by the lamp of gospel understanding, death is frequently viewed with fear and trembling. President Wilford Woodruff "referred to a saying of Joseph Smith, which he heard him utter (like this), That if the people knew what was behind the veil, they would try by every means to . . . get there. But the Lord in his wisdom had implanted the fear of death in every person that they might cling to life and thus accomplish the designs of their Creator."[7]

Strictly speaking, there is no death and there are no dead. When things die, they do not cease to be; they merely cease to be in this world. Life goes on. Death is a transition, a change in assignment, a transfer to another realm. When we die, the spirit continues to see and act and feel and associate; it is only the physical body that becomes inactive and lifeless for a season. And so it is that we use the term *death* to describe things as they seem to be from our limited perspective. From an eternal vantage point, however, there is only life.

I sat beside my father only a few hours before his death. He knew, and I knew, that a chapter in his eternal journey was coming to a close. There was a yearning in my soul to communicate—no, to commune—with him about sacred things, about things that matter most. We spoke at length about home and family and temples and covenants and sealings and eternal life. We expressed our love to each other and brought to an end, at least for a season, a sweet association, one that I look forward to resuming even more than I can say. I knew that I would miss him, that our family, especially my mother, would mourn his loss, and that it would be impossible to completely fill the void left by his passing. And yet there was no doubt whatsoever, in his heart or mine, that Albert Louis Millet would continue to live, for he was only about to be transferred to another field of labor. I was totally at peace during those tender moments, and that consummate assurance continued through his death and funeral. It continues to this day, after more than two decades. It is a peace born of perspective, a peace undergirded by the doctrine of life beyond the grave. It is a peace that derives from that Spirit who confirms that what my father had taught me through the years relative to life after death was indeed true.

These are not ideas that a really ingenious group of

people sat around and thought up. Instead, they are doctrines of consolation that come to us because of who Jesus Christ is and what he has done. Because Christ rose from the dead, so shall we. Had there been no Atonement, no hope of resurrection, death would remain an awful mystery and a horrible tragedy. But because of Jesus Christ, we view death with an elevated perspective, a perspective born of the Spirit, enlightened by scripture, and reinforced by living apostles and prophets. Had Jesus remained in the tomb, each of us would likewise be forever captive to death and our spirits would have remained a prisoner to Satan, the father of all lies (2 Nephi 9:8–9). "But thanks be to God, [who] giveth us the victory through our Lord Jesus Christ" (1 Corinthians 15:57).

"As mortals we all must die," President Gordon B. Hinckley explained. "Death is as much a part of eternal life as is birth. Looked at through mortal eyes, without comprehension of the eternal plan of God, death is a bleak, final, and unrelenting experience. . . .

"But our Eternal Father, whose children we are, made possible a far better thing through the sacrifice of His Only Begotten Son, the Lord Jesus Christ. This had to be. Can anyone believe that the Great Creator would provide for life and growth and achievement only to snuff it all into oblivion in the process of death? Reason says no. Justice demands a better answer. The God of heaven has given one. The Lord Jesus Christ provided it."[8]

We could go on and on, listing one question after another to which Jesus Christ is the undeniable answer. Yes, Jesus is the answer. He is the answer to all the serious questions through all the ages. Life has meaning because of him. Life has purpose because of him. We know who we are, Whose we are, why we are here, and where we are going because of him. He lives, he has spoken, he now speaks, and he will yet speak to those whose ears are attuned to the still, small voice. Because of him, no obstacle to peace and contentment here or to eternal life hereafter is too great to overcome.

Chapter 4
"JESUS LOVES ME, THIS I KNOW"

When a great Protestant theologian by the name of Karl Barth, a man who had spent his entire professional life reflecting and writing on the life and labors of Jesus Christ, visited the University of Chicago, a questioner asked, "Dr. Barth, what is the most profound truth you have learned in your studies?"

Most of us would have found that a difficult question to answer. How do you decide what is the most significant aspect of a lifetime of study? How do you determine what matters most?

Yet Dr. Barth quickly responded, "Jesus loves me, this I know, for the Bible tells me so."[1]

When I started school at five years of age, my family was not active in the Church. My mother was at the time a Methodist and my father, though raised as a Latter-day Saint, had slipped into the ranks of the less active. Consequently, when we moved to an area where we could not readily find an LDS chapel, my parents enrolled me in a local vacation Bible school. I have very sweet and positive memories of that experience and felt loved by my leaders and teachers. This was the first time I learned to sing "Jesus loves me, this I know, for the Bible tells me so" or, as the chorus has it, "Yes, Jesus loves me; yes, Jesus loves me; yes, Jesus loves me; the Bible tells me so."

My theological background is a bit stronger now in my life, and I know a few things at this point that I didn't know at age five, but I'm still moved by the profundity of that simple song. I now know from the Book of Mormon that Jesus loves me. I know it from the Doctrine and Covenants. I know it from the Pearl of Great Price. And I know it from the inspired teachings of Church leaders. I have also come to appreciate much more what must be the most frequently quoted scripture in religious history: "For God so loved the world, that he gave his only begotten Son, that whosoever believeth in him should not perish, but have everlasting life" (John 3:16), or, as John later writes, "He that loveth not knoweth not God; for God is love. In this was manifested the love of God toward us, because that God sent his only begotten Son into the world, that we might live through him"; truly, "we love him, because he first loved us" (1 John 4:8–9, 19).

Who can comprehend the work of a God? What finite being can fathom the ministerial labors of the Infinite One? We probably will never come to understand in this life the particulars of how the Savior took upon him the effects of the sins of all mortals; how Jesus of Nazareth engaged and bore the burden of all eternity; how the Master descended below all things. But there are some things we do know. Marvelous scriptural truths and prophetic utterances shed a glorious light upon what was surely the greatest act of submission and love in all eternity. Though it is to modern revelation that we turn for additional doctrinal understanding concerning the mediation of Jesus Christ, it is upon the New Testament, specifically the Gospels, that we rely for the details of the hours of atonement during our Lord's earthly ministry.

Having finished the Last Supper, the eleven apostles, with Jesus at their head, left the Upper Room. Mark records: "When they had sung an hymn, they went out into the mount of Olives" (Mark 14:26). East of the temple mount, outside the walls of the Holy City, on the slopes of the Mount of Olives was a garden spot, a place where "Jesus ofttimes resorted . . . with his disciples" (John 18:2)—Gethsemane, the garden of the oil press (or winepress). A lifetime of purity and preparation was now a part of the past. The hours of ordeal, the principal reason for which the Lord God Omnipotent had come to earth, were now at hand. It was a fateful occasion, transcendent in scope and incomprehensible to mortal minds; it was the hinge upon which the door into all eternity turned.

"They came to a place which was named Gethsemane, which was a garden; and the disciples began to be sore amazed, and to be very heavy, and to complain in their hearts, wondering if this be the Messiah. And Jesus knowing their hearts, said to his disciples, Sit ye here, while I shall pray" (JST, Mark 14:36–37). Elder Bruce R. McConkie wrote: "Though they all knew, as Jesus himself attested in the private sermons and prayer just delivered [the Intercessory Prayer in John 17], that he was the Son of God, yet he did not fit the popular pattern for the Jewish Messiah, and the disciples, of course, had not yet received the gift of the Holy Ghost, which means they did not have the constant companionship of that member of the Godhead."[2]

The time of anguish and alienation had begun. That for which the Lamb of God had been foreordained and that of which the prophets had spoken for millennia was under way. "When the unimaginable burden began to weigh upon Christ," Elder Neal A. Maxwell taught, "it confirmed His long-held and intellectually clear understanding as to what He must now do."[3]

No weight is heavier than the burden of sin, and the Sinless One (and those closest to him) began to sense and feel the bitterness of this singular occasion, a time when the weight of the world was about to be placed upon the shoulders of Him who had made the world. We must ever remember that Jesus was morally perfect. He had never taken a backward step or a moral detour. He was "in all points tempted like as we are, yet without sin" (Hebrews 4:15; compare 1 Peter 2:22). According to the Prophet Joseph Smith, Jesus was "the Son of God, and had the fullness of the Spirit, and greater power than any man."[4] He had never known the feelings of guilt and remorse, the pain of alienation from God that characterizes the whole of humankind.

There was a tragic irony surrounding this night of nights. He who had always pleased the Father (John 8:29) and had thus never been alone (that is, separated spiritually from his Father) was subjected to the forces and effects of sin that he had never known, forces that must have been poignantly and agonizingly intense. The God of the fathers, the Holy One of Israel, as he was known to the ancients, knew all things (2 Nephi 9:20). And yet there was something he had never known personally: he had not known directly either sin or its effects on the sinner. Christ knew all things as a spirit being; "nevertheless," Alma taught, "the Son of God suffereth according to the flesh that he might take upon him the sins of his people, that he might blot out their transgressions according to the power of his deliverance" (Alma 7:13). In the words of Elder Maxwell, "The suffering Jesus began to be 'sore amazed' (Mark 14:33), or, in the Greek, 'awestruck' and 'astonished.' Imagine, Jehovah, the Creator of this and other worlds, 'astonished'! Jesus knew cognitively what He must do, but not experientially. He had never personally known the exquisite and exacting process of an atonement before. Thus, when the agony came in its fulness, it was so much, much worse than even He with his unique intellect had ever imagined!"[5]

"He went forward a little, and fell on the ground, and prayed that, if it were possible, the hour might pass from him.

And he said, Abba, Father, all things are possible unto thee; take away this cup from me: nevertheless not what I will, but what thou wilt" (Mark 14:35–36). Removed from the apostles "about a stone's cast" (Luke 22:41), the Master pleaded in prayer. He called out in tender tones, "Abba," an intimate and familiar form of *father*, perhaps, as some scholars have suggested, something like "Papa." Was there not another way, he asked? It did not appear so. Could the plan of salvation have been operative without Jesus' selfless submission to the torturous experiences of the coming hours? It would seem not. We have no scriptural or prophetic indication that some substitute savior waited in the wings, some person who could fill in should Jesus of Nazareth not complete the task at hand. We sing with conviction: "There was no other good enough to pay the price of sin. / He only could unlock the gate of heaven and let us in."[6] No one else qualified for such an assignment. Earlier the Savior had spoken in soliloquy: "Now is my soul troubled," he had said, "and what shall I say? Father, save me from this hour: but for this cause came I unto this hour. Father, glorify thy name." The Father then spoke: "I have both glorified it, and will glorify it again" (John 12:27–28).

Luke wrote: "There appeared an angel unto him from heaven, strengthening him. And being in an agony he prayed more earnestly; and he sweat as it were great drops of blood falling down to the ground" (JST, Luke 22:43–44). An angel, sent from the courts of glory, came to strengthen the God of Creation in this hour of greatest need. "If we might indulge in speculation," Elder McConkie observed, "we would suggest that the angel who came into this second Eden was the same person who dwelt in the first Eden. At least Adam, who is Michael, the archangel—the head of the whole heavenly hierarchy of angelic ministrants—seems the logical one to give aid and comfort to his Lord on such a solemn occasion. Adam fell, and Christ redeemed men from the fall; theirs was a joint enterprise, both parts of which were essential for the salvation of the Father's children."[7]

Luke provided an additional detail concerning the intensity of our Lord's suffering, which was so great that drops of blood came to the surface of his body and fell to the ground (Luke 22:44). This was in fulfillment of the prophecy delivered by the angel to King Benjamin: "He shall suffer temptations, and pain of body, hunger, thirst, and fatigue, even more than man can suffer, except it be unto death; for behold, *blood cometh from every pore, so great shall be his anguish for the wickedness and the abominations of his people*" (Mosiah 3:7; italics added). In a modern revelation, the Savior pleaded with his people to repent, recalling the painful hours of atonement:

"I command you to repent—repent, lest I smite you by the rod of my mouth, and by my wrath, and by my anger, and your sufferings be sore—how sore you know not, how exquisite you know not, yea, how hard to bear you know not.

"For behold, I, God, have suffered these things for all, that they might not suffer if they would repent;

"But if they would not repent they must suffer even as I;

"Which suffering caused myself, even God, the greatest of all, to tremble because of pain, and to bleed at every pore, and to suffer both body and spirit—and would that I might not drink the bitter cup, and shrink—

"Nevertheless, glory be to the Father, and I partook and finished my preparations unto the children of men (D&C 19:15–19).

The immediate consequence of sin is the withdrawal of the Spirit (Alma 34:35). It may be that the withdrawal of the Spirit is what leads the individual to experience feelings of guilt and pain and emptiness. Jesus Christ, in taking upon him the effects of the sins of all humankind, was thus exposed to the awful (and to Jesus, unprecedented) withdrawal of that Spirit that had been his constant companion from the beginning. In speaking of the atoning mission of our Redeemer and the ordeals related to it, President Brigham Young explained:

"The Father withdrew His Spirit from His Son, at the time he was to be crucified. Jesus had been with his Father, talked with Him, dwelt in His bosom, and knew all about heaven, about making the earth, about the transgression of man, and what would redeem the people, and that he was the character who was to redeem the sons of earth, and the earth itself from all sin that had come upon it. The light, knowledge, power, and glory with which he was clothed were far above, or exceeded that of all others who had been upon the earth after the fall, consequently at the very moment, *at the hour when the crisis came for him to offer up his life, the*

Father withdrew Himself, withdrew His Spirit. . . . That is what made him sweat blood. If he had had the power of God upon him, he would not have sweat blood."[8]

Just as ancient Israel had sent the scapegoat into the wilderness (Leviticus 16:10), even so the Lamb of God, suffering outside Jerusalem's walls and outside the pale of God's healing and redemptive Spirit, faced the obstacles and assaults of Lucifer and his hosts. "In that hour of anguish Christ met and overcame all the horrors that Satan, 'the prince of this world,' could inflict. The frightful struggle incident to the temptations immediately following the Lord's baptism was surpassed and overshadowed by this supreme contest with the powers of evil."[9]

This was a night of irony. He who had come to impute or place on our account his righteousness had sin and evil imputed to his account. In Paul's words, God the Father had "made him to be sin for us, who knew no sin" (2 Corinthians 5:21). Paul taught the Galatian Saints that "Christ hath redeemed us from the curse of the law, being made a curse for us" (Galatians 3:13). He who deserved least of all to suffer, now suffered most—more than mortal mind can fathom. He who had brought life—the more abundant life (John 10:10)—was subjected to the powers of death and darkness. As the Prophet Joseph Smith taught, Jesus Christ "descended in suffering below that which man can suffer; or, in other words, suffered greater sufferings, and was exposed to more powerful contradictions than any man can be."[10]

Through most of our Lord's infinite ordeal, the chief

apostles slept. It is almost impossible to imagine that these noble and obedient servants of the Lord, called to be special witnesses of his name in all the world, could not control the demands of the body for a brief moment—indeed, a moment that mattered eternally. "Finite minds can no more comprehend how and in what manner Jesus performed his redeeming labors than they can comprehend how matter came into being, or how Gods began to be. Perhaps the very reason Peter, James, and John slept was to enable a divine providence to withhold from their ears, and seal up from their eyes, those things which only Gods can comprehend."[11]

The Atonement took place in Gethsemane and on Golgotha. What began in the garden was brought to its conclusion on the cross. President Ezra Taft Benson explained: "In Gethsemane and on Calvary, He [Christ] worked out the infinite and eternal atonement. It was the greatest single act of love in recorded history. Thus He became our Redeemer."[12] It was necessary that Jesus (1) forgive our sins and thereby deliver us from spiritual death; and (2) die and then rise from the dead, to offer the hope of resurrection, thereby overcoming physical death. One Book of Mormon prophet foresaw the time, some six hundred years ahead, when Jesus would be *"lifted up upon the cross and slain for the sins of the world"* (1 Nephi 11:33; italics added).

Thus our Savior descended below all things (Ephesians 4:8–10; D&C 88:6). The Redeemer has indeed "trodden the wine-press alone, even the wine-press of the fierceness of the wrath of Almighty God" (D&C 76:107; 88:106; see also

Isaiah 63:3). The miracle and blessings of the Atonement—timeless in their scope—continue to be extended to all who come to the Lord with righteous intent. "I am Christ," the Lord declared in a modern revelation, "and in mine own name, by the virtue of the blood which I have spilt, have I pleaded before the Father for them" (D&C 38:4). The nature of that pleading, that intercession, is spelled out in another revelation: "Listen to him who is the advocate with the Father, who is pleading your cause before him—Saying: Father, behold the sufferings and death of him who did no sin, in whom thou wast well pleased; behold the blood of thy Son which was shed, the blood of him whom thou gavest that thyself might be glorified; wherefore, Father, spare these my brethren that believe on my name, that they may come unto me and have everlasting life" (D&C 45:3–5).

Abinadi, in offering prophetic commentary on the greatest messianic chapter in the Old Testament (Isaiah 53), said of our Lord: "And thus the flesh becoming subject to the Spirit, or the Son to the Father, being one God, *suffereth temptation, and yieldeth not to the temptation,* but suffereth himself to be mocked, and scourged, and cast out, and disowned by his people" (Mosiah 15:5; italics added). To which temptation did Jesus refuse to yield? To all of them, you respond. Yes, the Savior was sinless, perfect, without flaw in his character. Other than the grand act of atonement itself, he was never required to forgive anyone because he had never taken personal offense at anyone. Imagine that!

But Abinadi seems to be referring to something more

specific, something far more subtle and infinitely more poignant. Our precious Redeemer refused to yield to the temptation—and it must have been a monumental one—to "not
drink the bitter cup," to stop when the going got roughest in
Gethsemane or on the cross, to refuse to finish his "preparations unto the children of men" (D&C 19:18–19). He didn't
have to do it. He had his agency. He could have backed
down, backed out, and backed away, but he did not. Why?
Because he loves us. I like to think that during those moments of temptation to call it quits, the Master might have
said, "No, I must go through with this. Bob Millet will need
me. And so will Beverly and Debra and Jack and Ernest" and
so on and so on.

He who had known us before we were even born came
to know us infinitely better as he knelt in Gethsemane and
as he hung on the cross of Calvary. We come to know those
we serve (Mosiah 5:13; compare 1 John 2:3–4). And we certainly come to love and treasure those for whom we sacrifice.
Conversely, the depth of the pain we feel in behalf of a loved
one is intimately tied to the depth of the love we feel for that
loved one. Thus only a being filled with infinite and eternal
love could perform an infinite and eternal sacrifice.

Indeed, we ask again the question we posed earlier: Who
can comprehend the work of a God? Nephi was asked if he
knew (or understood) the "condescension of God," how the
Messiah would be born of a virgin and be the Son of God;
how he would go forth among men and women teaching and
healing and blessing; and how he would be lifted up on the

cross and slain for the sins of the world. Nephi was no ig-
norant man, no novice in grasping eternal things. But he
was a humble man, a meek and mild man who knew very
well what he knew and acknowledged readily what he did
not. Nephi's answer to the angel was short but telling, for
it focused on the truth of truths, the message of messages:
"*I know that [God] loveth his children;* nevertheless, I do not
know the meaning of all things" (1 Nephi 11:16–17; italics
added; see also verses 18–33).

That is the beginning and the end of it all: God loves
his children. He loves you. And he loves me. God the Son
spoke in a modern revelation to Orson Pratt: "My son Orson,
hearken and hear and behold what I, the Lord God, shall say
unto you, even Jesus Christ your Redeemer; the light and the
life of the world, a light which shineth in darkness and the
darkness comprehendeth it not; who so loved the world that
he gave his own life, that as many as would believe might
become the sons of God" (D&C 34:1–3). That precious
principle is foundational to the plan of salvation, fundamental to the Atonement, and central to any progress we make
in this life or in the life to come.

Chapter 5

HOW GOOD
DO I HAVE TO BE?

I have been around only a little more than sixty years, but I believe that the Latter-day Saints today are more scripturally literate and more devoted to the faith than ever before. I well remember growing up in Louisiana in small branches and wards in which it was not uncommon to have only about 20 percent of the members attend sacrament meeting and a similar proportion visited by ward (home) teachers. Frankly, those statistics were not at the time very different from those for the overall Church. So, in many ways we have reason to rejoice that the gospel has taken hold in the lives of millions of people and is now moving quietly but surely throughout the earth.

The prophets and apostles have themselves indicated to the Saints that we are doing well, that in general we are on track, that such indicators as attendance at church meetings, payment of tithes, and participation in humanitarian efforts have been on the rise for many years. But are we where we need to be? We certainly do not want to slip into the attitude that Nephi warned about in which we find ourselves saying, "All is well in Zion; yea, Zion prospereth" (2 Nephi 28:21). Why? Because eventually, through our adopting this type of attitude, the devil will cheat our souls and lead us carefully down to hell. Well, then, what's the goal? How much more do I need to do? How much closer to the Lord do I need to be? How good is really good? How good do I need to be?

Righteousness and pure religion are not just about doing things, even a lot of good things. When we are called upon to stand before "the keeper of the gate," "the Holy One of Israel" (2 Nephi 9:41), I doubt that we will be required to witness our good deeds as they are weighed in the balance against our rebellion, sloth, and sin. Can't you see it now? "Come on, come on, one more good deed. Wasn't there one more noble action? I just need one more to get into the celestial kingdom." Maybe the reason this sounds rather silly is that in our heart of hearts we really do realize that what matters is the heart. In other words, while what we do certainly matters to God—we are called to be obedient disciples, to take up our cross daily, to deny ourselves of ungodliness, to follow him (Luke 9:23)—the real issue is, What are we *becoming*?

Here's another question, a peculiar one, but one that can be a bit sobering: What would I do if no one could see me? How would I conduct my life if, like Frodo Baggins, I could slip on a ring and become invisible? What if my parents, my teachers, my leaders, and even my friends couldn't see what I was doing, good or bad? Would my actions be any different if I were invisible? Now let's make the question even more interesting: What if no one could see me, *not even God?* That is, what if I could say or do anything I chose with the confident understanding that my attitudes and actions were known only to me? What if I were left to myself without any human or divine influence (including the Holy Spirit) and I were allowed to simply live according to my whims and wishes? How differently would I act?

True righteousness is not just measured in what we do, although what we do may be an indicator of our inner righteousness. True righteousness is what we have become, what we are, who we are. Elder Dallin H. Oaks taught that the process of becoming more like our Savior "requires far more than acquiring knowledge. It is not even enough for us to be *convinced* of the gospel; we must act and think so that we are *converted* by it. In contrast to the institutions of the world, which teach us to *know* something, the gospel of Jesus Christ challenges us to become something." Elder Oaks went on to say that "the Final Judgment is not just an evaluation of a sum total of good and evil acts—what we have *done.* It is an acknowledgment of the final effect of our acts and thoughts—what we have become." He continued: "It is not enough for anyone just to go through the motions. The commandments, ordinances, and covenants of the gospel are not a list of deposits required to be made in some heavenly account. The gospel of Jesus Christ is a plan that shows us how to become what our Heavenly Father desires us to become."[1]

President Spencer W. Kimball declared: "Now, my brothers and sisters, it seems clear to me, indeed, this impression weighs upon me—that the Church is at a point in its growth and maturity when we are at last ready to move forward in a major way. Some decisions have been made and others pending, which will clear the way, organizationally. But the basic decisions needed for us to move forward, as a people, must be made by the individual members of the Church. The major strides which must be made by the Church will follow upon the major strides to be made by us as individuals." He then added: "We have paused on some plateaus long enough. *Let us resume our journey forward and upward.*"[2]

President Gordon B. Hinckley similarly counseled us to "stand a little taller, to lift our eyes and stretch our minds to a greater comprehension and understanding of the grand millennial mission of this The Church of Jesus Christ of Latter-day Saints. This is a season to be strong. It is a time to move forward without hesitation, knowing well the meaning, the breadth, and the importance of our mission." President Hinckley added the comforting assurance that "We have nothing to fear. God is at the helm. He will overrule for the good of this work. He will shower down blessings upon those who walk in obedience to His commandments. Such has been His promise. Of His ability to keep that promise none of us can doubt."[3]

Life is not really a constant vertical climb. The process of spiritual growth and maturity seems to be one of climbing, pausing for rest and refreshment and reassurance, and then resuming the climb, on and on to the top. I am convinced that if we will seriously call upon the Lord and ask him regularly to bless us to feel what we ought to feel and see what we ought to see, we will sense the divine hand upon our shoulder, nudging us onward and upward, all the days of our lives. We will then begin to balance the divine discontent (a constant inner enticement to repent and improve) with what Nephi called "a perfect brightness of hope" (2 Nephi 31:20) and thereby find peace and lead happy and productive lives.

We cannot afford to rest apparently secure in our present condition of spirituality. I am persuaded from many years of experience in Church leadership that few people can actually pause on spiritual plateaus for long before they begin to lose the light they had and yield to the slow, almost imperceptible, decline that comes from complacency.

Just how bold are you? How open are you to divine correction or suggestion? Are you bold enough to ask the Lord as the young lawyer did, "What lack I yet?" (Matthew 19:20). Are you prepared to ask the question that the blinded Saul of Tarsus asked of the risen Lord: "Lord, what wilt thou have me to do?" (Acts 9:6).

I remember well kneeling in prayer at the end of a productive and Spirit-filled Sabbath. It had been a wonderful day, a day filled with worship, service, learning, and fellowship. Spiritually speaking, I was feeling on top of the world. I found myself saying to the Lord in prayer beside my bed that night, "Lord, what would you have me to do? I feel really good and feel like my life is, for the most part, on course. Is there anything in particular you would like me to work on, anything that needs some slight adjustment?"

I didn't have to stay on my knees very long before it seemed like the heavens had been rent and the spiritual floodgates had been opened. Within a few moments there came into my mind and heart the sobering realization that there were many, many things that needed "adjustment" in my life, several areas of refinement, improvement, and plain old repentance that were desperately needed.

This shouldn't have been surprising to me, for the Lord, speaking through Moroni had stated very plainly in the Book of Mormon: "And if men come unto me I will show unto them their weakness. I give unto men weakness that they may be humble; and my grace is sufficient for all men that humble themselves before me; for if they humble themselves before me, and have faith in me, then will I make weak things become strong unto them" (Ether 12:27).

I knew that scripture only too well, and I thought I understood its implications. First and foremost, it teaches us that if we will plead to the Lord for understanding concerning ourselves he will teach us, above and beyond everything else, of our weakness—our mortality, our fallenness, our limitations, and our absolute need for divine assistance. There is no question but that the Lord will also make known unto us our *weaknesses*, the specific areas in our life that are out of order and need immediate attention. Please remember that this is not the revelation of a harsh and vengeful god to his pitiful children but rather a kind and generous offering of an all-loving Being who wants more than anything for us to be all that we are intended to be.

It has become clear to me that many of us confuse means with ends, and in the process of doing so trip over priorities and lose track of things that matter most. Some have been brought up to believe that a full-time mission is, in a sense, a great end. Some come to believe that a temple marriage is a great end in life, something we prepare ourselves for years to achieve. Now, to be sure, missions and marriage are deeply significant moments in one's eternal journey, for they lay a foundation for life here and hereafter. But they are only a moment, a foundation upon which we must build our houses of faith. They are not ends in themselves but rather means to a greater end. When members of the Church view them as ends, we should not be surprised that they eventually ask aloud or in their hearts about their lives to that point, "Is this all there is?"

Those matters that receive the greatest focus in the Church—covenants, ordinances, temples, even families—are means to an end. They have been given to us by a gracious God to enable and empower us to "come unto Christ, and be perfected in him" (Moroni 10:32; see also D&C 20:59). We go to church, serve others, search the scriptures, fast and pray, participate in the ordinances of the temple, all in an effort to bridge the chasm between us and the heavens, to gain fellowship with our Heavenly Father and his Son Jesus Christ (1 John 1:3).

We teach and we listen, we minister and we receive counsel, we serve long hours in our callings and assignments, all to the end that we might grow up in the Lord and eventually "receive a fulness of the Holy Ghost" (D&C 109:15). Above and beyond all else, we strive to come to know God.

It is a long path, a strait path, a mountainous path that winds and curls and ascends, a journey that requires faith and energy and perseverance to reach the top. There are intermediate stops along the way, summits and plateaus that provide temporary rest and reassurance. But the climbers will not find ultimate satisfaction unless they are pressing toward the top of the mountain. And so it is with life.

There's a natural tendency in most of us to compare ourselves with other people, to say things like, "I wish I were as good as Becky" or "I feel like I'm trying my best to live the gospel, but I'm not even in the same spiritual ballpark with Charles." We must keep in mind always that our Heavenly Father does not grade on a curve. He does not and will not compare his children in terms of their individual righteousness or sinfulness. And aren't we grateful for that?

Popular Evangelical pastor Andy Stanley wrote: "What if God's holiness and perfection outweigh his mercy and he requires that 90 percent of our deeds be good? Or what if God grades on a curve and Mother Teresa skewed the cosmic curve, raising the bar for good deeds beyond what most of us are capable of?"[4] Inasmuch as each one of us makes mistakes, takes spiritual detours, commits sins, each one of us is in desperate need of pardoning mercy. Repentance is, or should be, a significant part of our daily lives, for in many ways life is repentance. Improvement is repentance. Refinement is repentance. And so if God allowed into the highest degree of the celestial kingdom only those who were free from sin, it would be a sizeable bunch of people but made up only of Jesus and little children. Thus the kind of people who go to heaven are not persons who have never sinned but rather persons who have fully repented of their sins. In short, *forgiven* people go to heaven.[5]

Two scriptural passages for many years were troublesome to me as I contemplated what I must do to become worthy of the celestial kingdom. The first one is found in the Book of Mormon and is an expression of King Benjamin's people following his marvelous discourse. His followers are deeply moved, touched to the core, have undergone a "mighty change" of heart, believe all that he has said, and announce publicly that they "have no more disposition to do evil, but to do good continually" (Mosiah 5:2). Wow! How would it be? Can you imagine not ever wanting to do anything wrong again? My guess is that there have been many times when you have been a part of an inspiring meeting or engaged in fervent prayer and the Spirit of the Lord came upon you and you found yourself expressing either aloud or to yourself, "I don't ever want to do anything wrong again. I just want to be good."

That is what the people of Benjamin were experiencing. Do we have any evidence to suggest that these people never sinned again? Certainly not. We would suppose that though their lives were changed dramatically, they still would be subject to temptation and as humans prone to make mistakes. No, they sinned again, *but they didn't want to!* Herein is the difference between the natural man or woman and the spiritual man or woman: the former wants to do wrong, whereas the latter wants to do right; their hearts are pointed in different directions. It isn't just that the people of Benjamin suddenly became more disciplined in their deeds, but rather they acquired a new *disposition,* an attitude that pointed them toward the righteous life.

The second passage that bothered me is found in the New Testament. In his first epistle, the apostle John states that those who are born of God do not commit sin (1 John 3:9). I read that passage many, many times, wondering what John meant. I knew people who had been born of the Spirit, who had tasted of the sweet fruits of the mighty change, but they weren't perfect. Indeed, I found myself acknowledging that I had been born again in regard to many matters, but I knew very well I was not perfect. Joseph Smith's translation of this passage makes a vital adjustment: We are taught that the person who is born of God "doth not continue in sin" (JST, 1 John 3:9; see footnote *b* to KJV 1 John 3:9). That's a different world entirely.

Spiritually reborn men and women cannot remain in a sinful condition. They have walked in the light and felt its magnificence, and so when they step momentarily into the darkness they feel extreme discomfort and desire only to get back into the light. They repent quickly (D&C 109:21) and find themselves reinstated in God's favor and once more walking the gospel path. Both of these scriptures, in other words, address themselves to the need to have our hearts changed, our direction changed, our orientation changed, and our perspective changed. In plain words, as we grow in the things of the Spirit we find ourselves enticed more by goodness than by evil.

How good do I need to be? My trust in the Lord Jesus Christ, my reliance upon his merits and mercy and grace, and my poor efforts to keep myself unspotted from the sins of the world—these things enable me to enjoy the gift and gifts of the Holy Ghost. I think we have not fully appreciated just how significant this spiritual endowment is. President Wilford Woodruff stated that while eternal life is the greatest of all the gifts in eternity, the gift of the Holy Ghost is the greatest of all the gifts of God in this life.[6] The Spirit in our life is God's sweet certification to us that we're on course, in covenant, and in line eventually to receive eternal life. The Holy Spirit is God's down payment to us, his "earnest money" on us, his indication that he seriously intends to save us with an everlasting salvation (2 Corinthians 1:21–22; 5:5; Ephesians 1:13–14).

One of my colleagues who served as a mission president

years ago taught his elders and sisters a principle that served them well, one that still echoes in my mind every day. This became their motto: "I would never do anything that would cost me the influence of the Spirit of the Lord." Such an ideal, such a standard, can work miracles in keeping us on the strait path and thus in line for eternal rewards hereafter. We strive to do our best, it is true, but it is worth knowing and acknowledging that *our best will not be enough;* we must have help. And we rejoice in the knowledge—a doctrine that is indeed the burden of scripture—that Jesus Christ came into the world to save sinners, to rescue and redeem people like you and me, to make up the difference, to make all the difference, and thus to make us different.

Chapter 6
THAT'S NOT FAIR!

During the process of trying to rear our children, many times Shauna and I did something for one of them that had not been done for the others; this was especially true for the younger ones. The older children would say something like, "Wait a minute! You can't do that. You didn't do that for me. That's not fair!" For years we cast about for some explanation of why we had chosen to give a gift to one of our offspring and not to another. "Yes," we would quickly respond, "but remember what we did for you when . . ." In other words, we hastened to assure the offended parties that we as parents handled everything in an orderly, systematic, even-handed, and thus appropriate manner with our children and that to suggest that we had somehow been unfair in our actions was preposterous.

As time passed and as the family grew, I wearied of the juggling act and gradually became less and less interested in defending my seemingly unfair practices. I still remember allowing one of the younger children who had just turned sixteen years of age and qualified for a driver's license to take the car quite a bit more frequently than we had allowed the older kids. One son asked, "Dad, why would you do that? You never let me take the car as much as you let him take it. It's just not fair!" Weary of explaining, I turned to the envious one and said simply, "Well, let me get right to the point of your question. I obviously love him more than I love you. I trust him a whole bunch more than I trusted you when you first received your driver's license. Does that make sense?"

The expression on his face reflected puzzlement, stupor of thought, amazement. Then he smiled, punched my arm, and we both laughed about it. The older boy knew that what I had just said was silly, even ridiculous. He knew his parents well enough to know that he was loved and cared about deeply and that we really didn't shower more affection on one child than on any of the other five. He recognized that I clearly did not want to deal with the age-old issue of fairness, nor did I want to take the time to justify and prove our consistency in working with each child. It really wasn't about fairness at all.

Try the following scenario. What if you enrolled for a college course in art history. The instructor was bright, energetic, charismatic, and fun. The information in his lectures was excellent, and his sense of humor and overall manner of presentation made the time zip by. What if, however, there was no course syllabus, no class outline, no predetermined dates for when a given topic would be covered, and, even more pertinent, no indication whatsoever when the quizzes and exams would be given? Now how would you feel about the class? You loved the learning environment, to be sure, but you were never quite certain what to study when or how or when to prepare for the teacher's evaluations. Is it conceivable that someone in the class might raise a hand and indicate that such an approach to the course was unfair? No doubt about it. But would it really be unfair? Awkward, unusual, even inconsiderate—it would be all of those things. But unfair? Does the instructor not have the right to teach what he will when he wants to? Does he not have the right to give quizzes or exams when he chooses? Are students not expected to come to each class prepared?

We live in a cause-effect world, in a sphere where we expect certain consequences to follow automatically from certain actions. For example, in the summer of 2001 I was in excellent physical condition. For six or seven years I had tried to eat a low-fat diet, avoid sweets, and to engage in hour-long aerobic exercise six days a week. That summer while helping one of my sons and his wife lay sod at their new home I was stricken with a serious heart attack, one that by all rights should have taken me into the spirit world. The weeks that followed were painful, taxing, and frustrating, as I sought to regain a measure of my strength and return to my daily activities. It never once occurred to me to say to God, "Wait a minute. I've grown up in the Church, gone on a mission, married in the temple, and served faithfully in my callings.

I've spent my life trying to live the gospel and teach the gospel to the best of my abilities. I'm not perfect (as everyone knows), but I am a decent sort of fellow who certainly deserves better than this. Besides all that, I'm in better physical shape than I have been in for twenty-five years. What's going on? This is *not* fair!"

Why didn't I get angry, shake my fist at God, and ease into an extended silent treatment of him? Because I know that I am a mortal, and this is a fallen world. Things break down and wear out. People contract cancer or dementia or diabetes or heart disease. It comes with the turf. Life isn't all about fairness; to use a few old-fashioned phrases, we learn to play with the hand that is dealt us, to roll with the punches, to move on. The idea of fairness is not a bad one, especially as each of us desires to have good returned for good and our best efforts rewarded. Sometimes, however, the notion of fairness gets in our way, prevents us from grasping much more profound and eternally relevant concepts, namely, such supernal principles as mercy and grace.

Jesus was famous for telling stories that contain what many would describe as an unfair message. For example, the parable of the prodigal son (Luke 15:11–32) seems to be one of the most unfair episodes in all of scripture. The younger brother gets the wanderlust, demands his inheritance, leaves home, and squanders his money on trivia and sin. Finding himself in the gutter—literally, feeding the pigs and possibly feeding with them—he thinks back on how good he had it at home and decides to return. And what happens? Do Mom and Dad open the door, look at him askance, and say, "What are you doing here? We thought you were gone for good." Does Dad say, "Well, you can stay for a few days until you can find a job and get out on your own. But don't get too comfortable here"? Do the wounded parents welcome him with such words as, "Let's don't get too cozy just yet. You prove yourself for the next several months and we'll talk"? All of these are perfectly human responses and perhaps the way many of us would be prone to act. We know only too well the roller coaster of emotions associated with a wanderer—the crushed expectations, the dashed hopes, the broken hearts.

In the parable, however, the father of the prodigal acts in a stunningly unusual manner: He welcomes his beloved son back with hugs and kisses, with a robe, a ring, a fatted calf, and a banquet to celebrate his return. But the older brother—the "faithful one"—is upset by the welcome. What he cannot see, through his green eyes, is that he is just as much a prodigal as his younger brother, only in different ways: He is the good boy with the bad heart. His snooty judgmentalism signals that his heart is not right, that the love and joy that ought to exist toward a loved one who finally comes to himself is sadly and tragically absent. We can almost hear the older brother cry out to his father, "What? You're doing what? I don't believe this. This is not fair!" He is right: it is not fair. But it is merciful and kind; it is gracious and tender. It is the right thing to do.

Why was the older brother angry? "You know the conversation [the father and older son] then had," noted Elder

Jeffrey R. Holland. "Surely, for this father, the pain over a wayward child who had run from home and wallowed with swine is now compounded with the realization that this older, wiser brother, the younger boy's childhood hero as older brothers always are, is angry that his brother has come home.

"No, I correct myself. The son is not so much angry that the other has come home as *he is angry that his parents are so happy about it.* Feeling unappreciated and perhaps more than a little self-pity, this dutiful son—and he is *wonderfully* dutiful—forgets for a moment that he has never had to know filth or despair, fear or self-loathing. He forgets for a moment that every calf on the ranch is already his and so are all the robes in the closet and every ring in the drawer. . . .

"No, he who has virtually everything, and who has in his hardworking, wonderful way earned it, lacks the one thing that might make him the complete man of the Lord he nearly is. *He has yet to come to the compassion and mercy, the charitable breadth of vision to see that this is not a rival returning. It is his brother.* As his father pled with him to see, it is one who was dead and now is alive. It is one who was lost and now is found."[1]

Similarly, the parable of the laborers in the vineyard (Matthew 20:1–16) teaches a timeless lesson. Some of the laborers who had been working all day long receive the agreed-upon salary, while others who began later in the day (some in the "eleventh hour") receive the same wage. The former group murmured to the employer about the seeming unfairness of the whole thing. "But he answered one of them, and said, Friend, I do thee no wrong: didst not thou agree with me for a penny? Take that thine is, and go thy way: I will give unto the last, even as unto thee. Is it not lawful for me to do what I will with mine own? Is thine eye evil, because I am good?" (Matthew 20:13–15).

We must ask ourselves, How would I feel if I had begun work in the vineyard at 6:00 A.M.? At 11:00 A.M.? At 3:00 or 5:00 P.M.? How would the others feel? We are reminded by one Christian writer, that "everyone receives the same amount, even the ones who started picking while dew was still on the grapes, who worked through scorching heat, who tore their hands and nearly broke their backs."[2] Protestant scripture commentator Robert Capon suggested that "this goes down like Gatorade for the last bunch hired, like dishwater for the next-to-the-last, like vinegar for the almost-first, and like hot sulfuric acid for the first-of-all."[3]

Elder Dallin H. Oaks pointed out that "the Master's reward in the Final Judgment will not be based on how long we have labored in the vineyard. We do not obtain our heavenly reward by punching a time clock. What is essential is that our labors in the workplace of the Lord have caused us to *become* something. For some of us, this requires a longer time than for others. *What is important in the end is what we have become by our labors.* Many who come in the eleventh hour have been refined and prepared by the Lord in ways other than formal employment in the vineyard. These workers are like the prepared dry mix to which it is only necessary to 'add water'—the perfecting ordinance of baptism and the gift of the Holy Ghost. With that addition—even in the eleventh hour—these workers are in the same state of development and qualified to receive the same reward as those who have labored long in the vineyard."[4] For the Eternal Father to say to one of us that "All that I have is thine" in no way precludes any of the rest of us from inheriting and receiving the same reward of eternal life. There is no ceiling on the number of saved beings.

Insisting that everything be fair is closely associated with the foolish and ill-advised attitude of "I just want what I deserve." Really? Do we really want to receive hereafter what we deserve? The apostle Paul explained that "all have sinned, and come short of the glory of God" (Romans 3:23). He also wrote that "the wages of sin is death" (Romans 6:23). His apostolic colleague, James the brother of Jesus, likewise wrote that "whosoever shall keep the whole law, and yet offend in one point, he is guilty of all" (James 2:10). In our dispensation the Savior warned: "I the Lord cannot look upon sin with the least degree of allowance" (D&C 1:31; compare Alma 45:16). This is God's standard of righteousness; He who is holy and pure could not require less. Our prayer to the Almighty should be constant and repetitive: "May I *not* receive hereafter what I deserve, for because of my sins and my regular surrender to Satan, I deserve death and hell and endless torment."

We often speak of God's mercy and grace in the Church today, more now than ever before. But do we grasp it? Are we open to it? Have we yielded to it—our will, our independence, the old man or woman of sin? We are desperately in need of pardoning mercy; to receive mercy is *not to receive what we deserve*. We are desperately in need of grace; to receive grace is *to receive what we do not and could never of ourselves merit or deserve*—forgiveness of sins, the cleansing of our hearts, the resurrection from the dead, and glorification in the world to come.

Whenever Shauna and I go to the temple, I spend time in the celestial room looking at my wife through eternal lenses and asking over and over, "What did I do to deserve her?" Whenever our burgeoning family gets together to celebrate a birthday or a holiday or have an expanded family home evening, I find myself going quiet at some point, looking around, distancing myself momentarily from involvement, feeling a sweet and supernal joy, and asking what I possibly could have done to deserve the feelings that come when I look at my children, listen to my grandchildren, and realize that this is what life is all about? Whenever I stand before a congregation to bear witness of the Savior and teach his gospel from the scriptures, my emotions rise to the surface as I puzzle over how I ever could have qualified for such a privilege. I count these and ten thousand more such episodes as priceless gifts, acts of sheer grace on the part of an omniloving and gracious Lord. And I sense, though I would certainly never admit it, that this is simply not fair!

Jacob, son of Lehi, exulted, "O the wisdom of God, his mercy and grace! . . . O how great the goodness of our God"

(2 Nephi 9:8, 10). The Father's plan of salvation, the gospel of Jesus Christ, is not, strictly speaking, a plan of fairness. It is a system of mercy, an extension of grace. "In order to untangle us from the web we had spun for ourselves," Pastor Stanley taught: "[God] had to do something very unfair. He had to send his son to this earth to die for sins he didn't commit. *Is Christianity fair? It is certainly not fair to God.* Christians believe that God sent his son to die for your sins and mine. *Fairness would demand that we die for our own sins.* But the good news is that God opted for grace and mercy over fairness."[5]

You know, the more I think about it, the more grateful I am for our Heavenly Father's loving and tender choice, a choice that enables and empowers us to be who and what we could never, ever be on our own.

Chapter 7
HOW WE WORSHIP

As a young man growing up in the Church, I heard many
times through the years such greetings as this one spoken by a member of the bishopric conducting the sacrament
meeting:

"Brothers and sisters and friends, we welcome you to our
sacrament meeting today. We are met together to worship
the Lord and to be edified and strengthened for the coming
week."

I always thought such words were a nice gesture, a warm
and inviting statement, a declaration that made me glad I
had come to church. But I frequently wondered what it really
meant to "worship the Lord." When I thought of worship, I
pictured in my mind the ancient Israelites bowing down to
the golden calf or neighbors of the children of Israel making
strange offerings to some deity made of wood or stone. In
other words, I didn't understand in those early years what it

meant to worship God. The idea of worship was fascinating to me and spoke to something deep in my soul, but I would certainly have had difficulty explaining what it meant.

As the years passed, it began to occur to me that worship meant many things. Not long ago I sat with my wife in a clearing in a beautiful forest and gazed up at the starlit heavens. After we had reflected and conversed for some time on the vastness of the creation, our hearts and our discussion turned to the Creator. We found ourselves in awe of all that God had made, of how infinite and eternal he must be who had formed the heavens and the earth, and of the endless testimonies that the creation bears of an all-wise and all-powerful Being. We found ourselves, in other words, in the spirit of worship, of praise and thanksgiving to the One responsible for it all.

There have been times in my life when, while singing a particular hymn at church, I found myself overcome by emotion, almost silenced by the feelings of appreciation and awe I felt toward our Heavenly Father or his Beloved Son, Jesus Christ. While singing such hymns as "How Great Thou Art," "I Stand All Amazed," "I Believe in Christ," or "Come, Thou Fount of Every Blessing" I have felt my spirit soar, my mind expand, my love broaden, and my gratitude deepen and intensify.

Sometimes when listening to general conference or to an address by a member of my ward or a lesson from a Sunday School teacher, I find my mind racing and my heart pounding, my soul silently expressing thanks to a gracious Lord for the goodness and soothing impact of truth, pure diamond truth. Often while serving as a bishop or a stake president, I found myself counseling with persons who had been guilty of serious sin, listening and perceiving and discerning the depth of that individual's contrition and soul searching. While doing so, I have enjoyed an outpouring of love and compassion that only comes by a revelation from God, and during those times I have felt myself in tune with the Infinite and in a small measure ministering to them as the Great Physician would. I realized that in my puny efforts as an undershepherd I was enjoying something akin to worship. "The forms of worship are many," Elder Bruce R. McConkie has written. "Prayers, sermons, testimonies, gospel ordinances, attendance at church meetings, doing missionary service, visiting the fatherless and the widows in their afflictions, and a great many other things are all part of pure religion and true worship."[1]

"Inborn in every man," President Ezra Taft Benson declared, "is a strong instinct to worship—to look toward heaven. Man has a hereditary passion to worship. By nature man wants to find God and to worship Him in spirit and in truth. He cries out for contact with Him."[2] Similarly, President Spencer W. Kimball taught that "man is naturally a religious being. His heart instinctively seeks for God whether he reverences the sacred cow or prays to the sun or moon; whether he kneels before wood and stone images, or prays in secret to his Heavenly Father, he is satisfying an inborn urge. . . .

"There is pathos in the present struggle of heralded

theologians, shuffling their feet in the dark with sweat and toil, in their quest for something to satisfy their inborn needs of a God to worship, to admire, to love, to lean upon in perilous times. It is sad to see them groping their way through the darkness only to find nothing at the end of their trail. . . .

"If all the theologians, the great thinkers, the philosophers, and the so-called Christian atheists in their intensive and continuous search were coming to a unity of faith or doctrine, then the world would sit up and take notice, but when their ideas run from mythology to personality, from reality to vagueness, how can one have much respect for their claims[?]"[3]

Worship is more than a task, much more than duty, worlds more than mere actions. It is a state of being, an attitude, a mindset. The depth of our worship is directly tied to how we feel about God, about Jesus Christ, about the Holy Spirit. In a study I did recently on the word *worship*, I discovered that initially *worship* referred to "worthiness," that over time it came to mean a state of distinction, credit, and dignity, and it eventually came to connote respect and reverence. To fear God is not to shudder beneath his anger but to reverence and respect him. It is to worship him. Jesus Christ is our Exemplar in worship as in all things. I likewise feel tremendous gratitude for the Holy Ghost, the third member of the Godhead. He is a revelator, a teacher, a guide, a companion, an advocate, a comforter, a sanctifier, and a sealer. He bears witness of the Father and of the Son (3 Nephi 11:32, 36). In the words of Jesus, the Holy Ghost "shall not speak of himself; but whatsoever he shall hear, that shall he speak: and he will shew you things to come. He shall glorify me: for he shall receive of mine, and shall shew it unto you" (John 16:13–14).

It is clear that God our Eternal Father is the ultimate object of our worship (JST, John 4:26; D&C 18:40; 20:19). He is God the First, the Creator. He is the Father of the spirits of all humankind (Numbers 16:22; 27:16; Hebrews 12:9). The scriptures attest that people worshipped Jesus Christ, the Son of God, during his mortal ministry (Matthew 2:11; 8:1–2; 9:18–21; 14:22; 15:25; 28:9, 17; Mark 5:6; John 9:38; see also 2 Nephi 25:29; D&C 76:21), as well as during his postresurrection stay among his American Hebrews (3 Nephi 11:17; 17:10). We search the scriptures and strive to align ourselves with the Spirit of the Lord in order to better comprehend the character, perfections, and attributes of the members of the Godhead. Over time we find ourselves progressing from admiration to adoration to emulation to spiritual transformation.

Our feelings toward Jesus Christ cannot be separated from our feelings for our Heavenly Father. What would you think of a conversation among three Latter-day Saints sitting around in a circle and saying such things as "I reserve most of my feelings for the Father" or "Frankly, I'm more tied to the Son," or "I spend most of my time with the Spirit"? The reason such a conversation seems odd or inappropriate is that we do not separate the members of the Godhead: They are one, infinitely more one than they are separate. Elder Jeffrey R.

Holland has reminded us: "Our first and foremost article of faith in The Church of Jesus Christ of Latter-day Saints is 'We believe in God, the Eternal Father, and in His Son, Jesus Christ, and in the Holy Ghost' (Articles of Faith 1:1). We believe these three divine persons constituting a single Godhead are united in purpose, in manner, in testimony, in mission. We believe Them to be filled with the same godly sense of mercy and love, justice and grace, patience, forgiveness, and redemption. I think it is accurate to say we believe They are one in every significant and eternal aspect imaginable *except* believing Them to be three persons combined in one substance, a Trinitarian notion never set forth in the scriptures because it is not true."[4]

Many students through the years have asked me various forms of the following question: "How am I supposed to get close to Christ if I'm praying to my Heavenly Father?" We have been instructed to follow a pattern in our prayers: we pray to the Father, in the name of the Son, by the power of the Holy Ghost. That is the pattern that Jesus taught (John 14:13–14; 16:23–24; 3 Nephi 18:19–21; 19:6–8; Moroni 7:26). As we mature spiritually, we begin to feel a deeper closeness to the Father and the Son and a greater appreciation for the Holy Ghost, who testifies of both of them. We worship God, meaning the Godhead. We do not pick out one member of the Godhead on whom to shower our affections, nor do we pray or worship in any way contrary to the appointed pattern.

"I make my own heartfelt declaration of God our Eternal Father this morning," Elder Holland explained, "because some in the contemporary world suffer from a distressing misconception of Him. Among these there is a tendency to feel distant from the Father, even estranged from him, if they believe in him at all. And if they do believe, many moderns say they might feel comfortable in the arms of Jesus but they are uneasy contemplating the stern encounter with God. Through a misreading (and surely, in some cases, a mistranslation) of the Bible, these see God the Father and Jesus Christ His Son, as operating very differently. This in spite of the fact that in both the Old Testament and the New, the Son of God is one and the same, acting as he always does under the direction of the Father, who is himself, the same 'yesterday, today, and forever.'

"In reflecting on these misconceptions, we realize that one of the remarkable contributions of the Book of Mormon is its seamless, perfectly consistent view of divinity throughout that majestic book. Here there is no Malachi-to-Matthew gap, no pause while we shift theological gears, no misreading the God who is urgently, lovingly, faithfully at work on every page of that record from its Old Testament beginning to its New Testament end. Yes, in an effort to give the world back its Bible and a correct view of Deity with it, what we have in the Book of Mormon is a uniform view of God in all His glory and goodness, all His richness and complexity— including and especially as again demonstrated through a personal appearance of His Only Begotten Son, Jesus Christ." Elder Holland later observed that "Jesus did not come to improve God's view of man nearly so much as He came to improve man's view of God and to plead with them to love their Heavenly Father as He has always and will always love them."[5]

Latter-day Saints who search the scriptures and attend to the counsel of living apostles and prophets learn over time how to worship and Whom they worship. "We are happy in our knowledge that the God of this universe is a God of revelation," President Kimball observed. "Our Lord communicates his mind and will to his children on earth. If we seek it, he will reveal himself more and more and in greater and greater fullness, and we shall comprehend him as well as it is possible for mortal man to comprehend God. We cannot worship a being of our own creation or of the imaginations of our minds. We worship a being who lives, who has created, who communicates to us his character and his attributes and the greatness of his being."[6]

John the Revelator beheld in vision "ten thousand times ten thousand" beings lifting their voices heavenward in worshipful adoration: "Worthy is the Lamb that was slain to receive power, and riches, and wisdom, and strength, and honour, and glory, and blessing" (Revelation 5:11–12). And from our own hymnal we sing:

> *Glory to God on high!*
> *Let heaven and earth reply.*
> *Praise ye his name.*
> *His love and grace adore,*
> *Who all our sorrows bore.*

Sing aloud evermore:
Worthy the Lamb!

Jesus, our Lord and God,
Bore sin's tremendous load.
Praise ye his name.
Tell what his arm has done,
What spoils from death he won.
Sing his great name alone:
Worthy the Lamb!

Let all the hosts above
Join in one song of love,
Praising his name.
To him ascribed be
Honor and majesty
Through all eternity:
Worthy the lamb![7]

Chapter 8

"GENTLY RAISE
THE SACRED STRAIN"

A treasured friend and colleague, Paul H. Peterson, passed
away after a noble and courageous fight with cancer.
Paul had been a member of the Religious Education faculty
at Brigham Young University only a few years less than I had,
and he had worked in the Church Educational System for
even longer than I. He was a phenomenal man, a dear friend
to everyone, a man who indeed was no respecter of persons,
a transparent man of whom you could truly say, "What you
see is what you get." He had a charming personality, including a fun, self-deprecating manner that endeared him to students and colleagues alike. Paul and I spent scores of hours
together in gospel discussion, wrestling with this scriptural
passage and that one, tugging on this or that theological or
historical thought. Paul was admired and respected by his
peers, having served two terms as chair of the department
of Church History and Doctrine at BYU and two years as

director of the BYU Jerusalem Center. He worked for several years on our LDS-Evangelical dialogue team, and the love and esteem in which he was held by our Evangelical friends was also evident. Most important, he was loved and adored by his wife and children and grandchildren, and so his passing was a blow to all of us.

The funeral services were a marvelous spiritual experience. The Spirit bore record to each one in attendance that Paul was still very much alive, that he had only been transferred to another field of labor, and that the Lord had accepted his offering and would crown his sweet labors with eternal life. One tender feature of the funeral was that the Religion faculty had been asked to sing one of Paul's favorite hymns, "How Great Thou Art." Obviously we had all sung that magnificent hymn of praise and acknowledgment many, many times, but this time it was different: we were singing it at the request of Paul's family and with a complete realization that the message of that heavenly song had special meaning to our departed friend. As we sang, as we lifted up our united voices to proclaim God's magnificence, majesty, and tender mercy, we became aware that we were not singing alone, that we were being joined by strains and melodies and voices from just beyond the veil. We were participating in a celebration of a meaningful life. We were bidding a temporary farewell to a beloved friend, but, more important, we were praising the God and Father of us all, thanking him for his goodness, proclaiming his sovereignty, and surrendering and consecrating our souls to him and to his service. In short, we were worshipping.

We worship God when we praise God. Reflect upon the titles and words of some majestic hymns we sing:

"A Mighty Fortress Is Our God" (*Hymns*, no. 68)

"All Creatures of Our God and King" (*Hymns*, no. 62)

"For the Beauty of the Earth" (*Hymns*, no. 92)

"How Wondrous and Great" (*Hymns*, no. 267)

"Praise God from Whom All Blessings Flow" (*Hymns*, no. 242)

"Praise to the Lord, the Almighty" (*Hymns*, no. 72)

"Rejoice, the Lord Is King" (*Hymns*, no. 66)

"Sweet Is the Work, My God, My King" (*Hymns*, no. 147)

"Oh, May My Soul Commune with Thee" (*Hymns*, no. 123)

And on and on. I have felt in my own life the need to make a conscious effort in Church meetings to delight in song, especially in songs of praise, as a form of worship, as a prayer unto Deity (D&C 25:12). I have had to work at it, to make sure that when I am singing to the Lord, I realize that I am speaking to the Lord. Truly, a worship service is not a worship service for me if the congregation does not sing.

It matters little how trained one's voice is or even if one can carry a tune, if one's heart is genuinely offering up rejoicings to the heavens. I do not sing in church because I have a voice like Pavarotti or Andrea Bocelli or Josh Groban or Robert Peterson or Michael Ballam or Kenneth Cope, because (it goes without saying) I do not. I sing because it is a singular and significant part of my worship, because it contributes to the congregation's prayer to the Almighty. In addition, I sing because it allows me to shout out messages of the heart that my own words can utter in no other way.

"Inspirational music is an essential part of our church meetings," the First Presidency stated in the Preface to the 1985 hymnal. "The hymns invite the Spirit of the Lord, create a feeling of reverence, unify us as members, and provide a way for us to offer praises to the Lord.

"Some of the greatest sermons are preached by the singing of hymns. Hymns move us to repentance and good works, build testimony and faith, comfort the weary, console the mourning, and inspire us to endure to the end."[1]

Allow me to share one or two of a dozen stories I could tell of how singing unto God has transformed my heart and purified my motives. I received my call to serve a full-time mission during the 1960s, at a time when the Vietnam War was raging and the Selective Service Office was extremely attentive to the number of LDS young men leaving for missions, men who could just as well serve in the military. Through the inspired work of general Church leaders, many of us were allowed to postpone military obligations and serve our God for two years. It was a tense season, and timing was everything. The process could unfold incredibly rapidly. In my case, I was interviewed by my stake president on January 30, 1967, received my mission call in the mail on February 10th, instructing me to be at the Missionary Home in Salt Lake City ten days later on Monday, February 20th. Because it was a three- to four-day drive from Louisiana to Utah, there was little time to do anything other than shop and pack. No time to get my mind wrapped around what I was about to do. No time to say good-bye to all my friends. No time to think seriously about just how long twenty-four months is. No time to ask one of the most significant questions of all: Is this something I am prepared to do, something I am fully committed to do? I had always admired the missionaries and wanted to be just like them. I had always enjoyed sharing the gospel with my friends. But now, this—was I up to it?

I was scheduled to speak in sacrament meeting on Sunday evening, February 12th, to sign off, to put my social life on hold, to postpone education and training and a myriad of other things. More than anything I felt anxious—nervous and hurried and worried. The sacrament meeting began at 7:00 p.m. (as sacrament meetings did back then), and the messages by former Primary and Sunday School teachers and priesthood leaders (my dad was my bishop) were inspirational. I felt okay about what I said to the congregation as I expressed thanks and bore testimony. But I was not yet at peace. In fact, it was not until we sang the closing hymn that I felt the peace I longed for. It was a hymn I had sung frequently since I was a child, but now it took on new meaning for me. I felt the peace and power and perspective of the Lord make their way into my soul and provide solace to my being. Through my tears I surrendered my will:

It may not be on the mountain height
Or over the stormy sea,
It may not be at the battle's front
My Lord will have need of me.
But if, by a still, small voice he calls
To paths that I do not know,
I'll answer, dear Lord, with my hand in thine:
I'll go where you want me to go.[2]

It wasn't just the music that I knew so well, nor was it the words I had memorized from frequent use. Rather, I realized then and there that I was speaking to the One who had called me through a living prophet, President David O. McKay. It was a sweet and solemn occasion, a sanctifying and soothing moment, an expression of my acceptance of a divine call from him who sends his servants where they are needed. It was a moment that mattered, a moment of sober and soul-stirring worship. I have never been the same since.

Churches today, especially Christian churches, face a real challenge. They do whatever they can to attract and hold on to young people—to provide a place for them to gather, to deliver a message that is uplifting and edifying, and to thereby keep them from the sins of Sodom and Gomorrah that are on all sides. Thousands of churches have sought to meet this challenge by altering their style of music, by turning to contemporary Christian tunes, and by providing an entertaining environment. In some cases the music is still quite soft and sensitive, while in other cases the beat and rhythm of the music have become loud and hard. Lyrics have been simplified dramatically but are intended to speak of and to the Lord, to rejoice in his goodness and grace, and to surrender to his mercies. An Evangelical friend of mine described this "praise music" as 7/11 music, meaning there are seven words that are sung eleven times.

Not long ago I attended a worship service with a friend of another faith, a Friday evening worship service intended for youth. It was a two-hour meeting, of which about twenty or twenty-five minutes were taken up by an excellent and inspiring message from the pastor. His sermon was sound, solid, and scriptural, and the young people, about twelve hundred in number, seemed to identify with the principles he taught. This was a great group of kids, attending a kind of "come as you are" gathering, youth who appeared to love their Lord and were seeking to be fed the bread of life.

Most of the time was devoted to praise music, which was led by a band with electric guitar, bass guitar, piano, drums, and lead singer. The words to the songs were, once again, deferential and tender expressions of love to the Savior, but the music was hard and especially loud. As time passed, the intensity of the meeting rose, and the emotional electricity in the air reached a fever pitch. Young people on both sides of me were clapping their hands, jumping up and down, screaming, and even falling to the floor onto their knees in a posture of pleading prayer.

My heart went out to them. I loved them. I loved them for the righteous desires of their hearts. I loved them for the yearning in their souls to worship God. And I loved them for their choice of this way to spend an evening. But my heart was troubled.

I prayed. I prayed and prayed. I asked the Lord to open my mind, to dispel prejudice, to help me to discern between what was simply not my preference from what was not appropriate. I pleaded with my Father in Heaven to help me, a sixty-something who had grown accustomed to traditional sacred music, to rise above likes and dislikes and discern what was and what was not happening. Try as I might for more than an hour, I could not dispel the questions that rang in my ears over and over: Does this style of music contribute to the true spirit of worship? Does it invite and maintain the influence of the Spirit? Would Jesus himself be comfortable with it?

Professor John Stackhouse at Regent College wrote that what's wrong with such music is "what's wrong with—or at least limited about—pop music in general. Except for the very best, it generally hits you hard with a shot of pleasure, and then it leaves you physically and emotionally stimulated but intellectually and spiritually malnourished. Most of it is junk food: You don't need teeth to eat it, and there is nothing to digest. The moronic 'Baby, baby, love, love' of MTV gets baptized into 'Jesus, Jesus, love, love' with approximately the same effect: warm fuzzies.

"Now, I welcome my share of warm fuzzies," Stackhouse continued, "and I like a wide range of popular music. The best of it expresses basic feelings in primary—even neon—colors of the soul. The same can be said for the Christian versions of it. But Christians are not growing when their worship music is restricted to five-chord pop tunes, endlessly repeated choruses, and lyrics that—at best—contain interchangeable bits of Scripture with no obvious progression of thought."[3]

Turning to popular trends and gimmicks is not the way to tie our youth or our more seasoned members to the faith; we do not take our cues from the world. President Boyd K. Packer sounded a warning decades ago when he said: "I would remind all [of us] that it is not the privilege of those called as leaders to slide the Church about as though it were on casters, hoping to put it into the path that men or youth will be safe within it."[4]

I have great confidence in our youth of the noble birthright. I believe in their ability and their capacity to discern and to prioritize. I sense that they know when it is appropriate to sing more popular religious music in firesides or youth conferences or campouts, and when it is time to turn toward the hymns and anthems that through the centuries have brought us nearer to God, music that soothes and sanctifies the soul, music that serves as a catalyst to personal and group communion and that invites revelation, music that contributes to worship.

Several years ago Shauna and I went to the hospital to visit a dear friend who was seriously ill. Stan Farley had been our home teacher for many years in Orem, Utah, and we and our children welcomed his visits, which always contained a story from his own vast experience that enriched our lives.

I was serving as bishop of our ward at the time of his hospitalization and visited him as often as I could. It became clear that his days were numbered, that our beloved brother would not be with us much longer. He did not fear death, and he told us so. He indicated that he appreciated our visits very much but that he especially appreciated whenever his daughter-in-law Janine would come to visit and then sing to him. I asked what he enjoyed hearing most. With trembling lips and moist eyes he responded:

> More holiness give me,
> More strivings within,
> More patience in suff'ring,
> More sorrow for sin,
> More faith in my Savior,
> More sense of his care,
> More joy in his service,
> More purpose in prayer.[5]

Worshipping through music invites the Spirit of God, and the Spirit of God points us toward the reality of the unseen. We come to feel the power and influence of Jesus Christ as we sing of Jesus Christ. We think back upon him as the Exemplar, the Prototype of all saved beings, when we think of his ministry in the meridian of time, and thus we sing of wanting to be like Jesus. We are reminded of the infinite price the Master paid for us when we sing of his sufferings in the garden of Gethsemane and on the cross of Calvary.

We look with bright hope toward that grand day when righteousness will prevail and wickedness will be no more, and thus we sing of his coming again to reign on earth as King of kings and Lord of lords. Sacred music lifts our sights to loftier things. Worshipful music transforms us from time-bound and sin-laden persons to persons of faith, individuals of purpose and of power, individuals who want to know and be like Christ.

Chapter 9

THE IMITATION OF CHRIST

Primary children sing the tender and touching words, "I'm trying to be like Jesus."[1] Although I didn't sing that particular song as a child (it was yet to be written), I have had feelings akin to what the children sing for as long as I can remember. I've always wanted to be better than I am. I've always wanted to live in a way that would bring peace to my soul and a feeling of closeness to my Heavenly Father. It is no surprise, however, that I have often fallen short of my spiritual ambitions, have felt or spoken or acted in ways that were less than Christlike. Through the years I have tried to keep the commandments and attend my meetings and work at the stake farm and serve as a home teacher because I was afraid of what might become of me hereafter if I didn't. I have served in bishoprics and stake presidencies, read my scriptures and prayed, attended the temple, and even participated in pinewood derbies because it was my duty to do so. I

have fulfilled Church callings because of the sweet association I have enjoyed with good men and women who love the
Lord and stand as a noble example for me.

I don't suppose there's anything wrong with serving out
of fear of divine retribution, working hard out of a sense of
responsibility, or laboring alongside good people whose influence upon us is positive and uplifting. At this point in my
life, however, being much closer to the casket than to the
cradle, I find myself thinking more and more about God the
Father and his Son Jesus Christ, about how overwhelmingly
grateful I am to Them for the unspeakable blessings they
have showered upon me, and about how earnestly I want to
enjoy association with Them now and after I pass through
the veil of death. I no longer go home teaching because I am
fearful of what the high priests group leader or the bishop
might think or say if I do not. Most of the time I go because
I care deeply about the families assigned to me and I want to
see to their temporal and spiritual welfare. I rarely attend the
temple because of some external or even internal quota. I go
because I cannot help it; my soul cries out to sit and ponder
and pray and commune and covenant and worship in holy
places. In short, while I hope I have miles to go before I enter
my eternal rest, I can see that much of my motivation for
doing what I do has undergone a gradual and genuine transformation during my sixty-plus years on earth.

I remember quite well what it was like to be a Latter-day
Saint in a strong Baptist community. I had very few LDS
friends, except at church. And yet my friends of other faiths

were good people, youth who had been well taught and who for the most part behaved themselves. None of my close friends smoked or drank or took drugs, and they were pretty protective of me and my values—they wouldn't even allow me to have a Coke at the malt shop! Sadly, many of these friends changed when we moved into university life. Beer parties on Friday nights were the order of the day. Tobacco and marijuana and cocaine became part of their lives. Loose moral living followed closely thereafter. It was the 1960s, and everything was up for grabs. Besides, they maintained, there are no absolutes in life. I had never really known peer pressure during high school, but now the pressure began in earnest. I realized that I had a decision to make—not a series of decisions but rather one very large decision: will I or will I not change my standards to keep my friends? Mercifully, God be thanked, I chose the gospel path. I chose to say no. I chose to spend Friday nights alone sometimes. At home. I chose to deny myself what the crowd deemed the best things in life. They contended that the grass was much greener on the other side of the fence, but I came to understand over time that *the reason it was so green was that it was plastic!* It was fake. Empty. It was not real, nor was the life my friends had chosen.

I have often reflected since on why I did not choose the road most traveled, and my wife Shauna and I have discussed it a great deal over the years we have been married. Both of us can remember that our consciences were alive and well and warned us that such living would lead to a lengthy detour, to misery and pain, to a dead end. But we also remember what was probably the most significant variable in making our choices: we simply did not want to do anything that would disappoint our parents. We wanted them to be pleased with us, to feel that their wonderful and loving teaching had made a difference in how we chose to live our lives. We just couldn't let our folks down. That simple decision made all the difference.

I want to feel comfortable in holy places. I want to feel at ease around holy people. And one day, in the not too distant future, I want to feel delight in being ushered into sacred precincts beyond the veil. I want to feel confidence in the presence of the Lord (D&C 121:45). Alma asked the people of Zarahemla: "I say unto you, can you imagine to yourselves that ye hear the voice of the Lord, saying unto you, in that day: Come unto me ye blessed, for behold, your works have been the works of righteousness upon the face of the earth?" (Alma 5:16).

I *can* conceive of such an occasion, and it's a supernal anticipation. Enos, son of Jacob, closed his small book with this beautiful testimony: "And I soon go to the place of my rest, which is with my Redeemer; for I know that in him I shall rest. And I rejoice in the day when my mortal shall put on immortality, and shall stand before him; then shall I see his face with pleasure, and he will say unto me: Come unto me, ye blessed, there is a place prepared for you in the mansions of my Father" (Enos 1:27).

Eternal life is God's life. It is life in the highest heaven, a life in which we enjoy fellowship with God our Father, his Son, the Lord Jesus Christ, with members of our family, and with friends who have developed like passions for Christ and his gospel. Enjoying eternal life is therefore being *with* God. But it is even more, so very much more. It is a state of be-ing—being *like* God, having acquired many of his attributes and characteristics, having enjoyed the cleansing power of the Savior's blood, and having been sanctified by the Spirit, made pure and holy and completely comfortable to stand (or kneel) in the divine presence. Thus Amulek taught that "this life is the time for men to prepare to meet God; yea, behold the day of this life is the day for men to perform their labors" (Alma 34:32).

A modern revelation instructs us that our Lord and Master grew in spiritual graces ("from grace to grace") as he was willing to be inconvenienced, as he took the time to minister to the troubled, as he lifted the burdens of the suffering and liberated the captives from ignorance and sin (D&C 93:13). Then the Redeemer unveiled the lesson to be learned: "I give unto you these sayings, that you may under-stand and know how to worship, and know what [Whom] you worship, that you may come unto the Father in my name, and in due time receive of his fulness. For if you keep my commandments you shall receive of his fullness, and be glorified in me as I am in the Father; therefore, I say unto you, you shall receive grace for grace" (D&C 93:19–20; see also vv. 12–18).

The greatest evidence of our growth unto Christlikeness

is the extent to which we are coming to appreciate and love people, the extent to which we are beginning to bear the fruit of the Spirit—"love, joy, peace, longsuffering, gentleness, goodness, faith, meekness [poise under provocation], temperance [self control]" (Galatians 5:22–23). In other words, the way we treat other children of God is an unerring measure of how we're becoming more like God. We're no longer just talking the talk of a Latter-day Saint Christian; we're walking the walk. "If we live in the Spirit," Paul declared, "let us also walk in the Spirit" (Galatians 5:25).

Consider the following divine invitations and instruction:

"Be ye therefore perfect, even as your Father which is in heaven is perfect" (Matthew 5:48).

"Therefore I would that ye should be perfect even as I, or your Father who is in heaven is perfect" (3 Nephi 12:48).

"My little children, of whom I travail in birth again until Christ be formed in you" (Galatians 4:19).

"For who hath known the mind of the Lord, that he may instruct him? But we have the mind of Christ" (1 Corinthians 2:16).

"Whereby are given unto us exceeding great and precious promises: that by these ye might be partakers of the divine nature, having escaped the corruption that is in the world through lust" (2 Peter 1:4).

"Behold, what manner of love the Father hath bestowed upon us, that we should be called the [children] of God: therefore the world knoweth us not, because it knew him not. Beloved, now are we the [children] of God, and it doth not yet appear what we shall be [in the resurrection]: but we know that, when he shall appear, we shall be like him; for we shall see him as he is" (1 John 3:1–2; compare Moroni 7:48).

"Therefore, what manner of men ought ye to be? Verily I say unto you, even as I am" (3 Nephi 27:27).

In other words, we have been sent to earth to grow up, to mature in the things of the Spirit, the things of righteousness, and to acquire—through the atoning blood of Jesus Christ and by means of the Holy Spirit—Christlike, Godlike attributes and qualities. Above and beyond all that we are here to do, we are here to come to know God and Christ (John 17:3) and become like them. As popular Christian writer Max Lucado pointed out, "God loves you just the way you are, but he refuses to leave you that way. He wants you to be just like Jesus."[2]

Now to some extent the process of spiritual growth is a matter that is out of our hands because of the works of a gracious Savior, who is our change agent, who offers to renew us from the inside out. On the other hand, we can decide to bring to an end that season of our life in which we were trying pitifully and painfully to save ourselves. That decision is ours, for God will force no man to heaven.[3] Note the following passages:

"And [Jesus] said to them all, If any man will come after me, let him deny himself, and take up his cross daily, and follow me" (Luke 9:23).

"If any man will come after me, let him deny himself, and take up his cross, and follow me. And now, for a man to take up his cross, is to deny himself all ungodliness, and every worldly lust, and keep my commandments" (Matthew 16:24; see also footnote d).

"Yea, come unto Christ, and be perfected in him, and deny yourselves of all ungodliness" (Moroni 10:32).

The phrase rendered from the Greek as "deny himself" means to refuse to associate with, to decide to no longer tolerate, to distance ourselves from the natural man, the old man of sin. To come unto Christ is to have made the conscious decision—based upon past experience—that our old and spiritually outmoded ways of doing things simply do not cut the mustard. They do not work. They fall short. They take us beyond the mark. They are at best deficient and at worst perverse. They do not bring happiness and joy here or eternal salvation hereafter. In other words, when I have reached the point where I have become sick of the old life and yearn to be a new person with a new and improved future, at that moment I open myself to the transformation that comes automatically from yielding my heart to the Lord.

"The more you obey your conscience," C. S. Lewis observed, "the more your conscience will demand of you. And your natural self, which is thus being starved and hampered and worried at every turn, will get angrier and angrier. . . .

"Christ says 'Give me All. I don't want so much of your time and so much of your money and so much of your work: I want You. I have not come to torment your natural self, but to kill it. No half-measures are any good. I don't want to cut off a branch here and a branch there, I want to have the whole tree down. I don't want to drill the tooth, or crown it, or stop it, but to have it out. Hand over the whole natural self, all the desires which you think innocent as well as the ones you think wicked—the whole outfit. I will give you a new self instead. In fact, I will give you Myself: my own will shall become yours."[4]

Isn't that what Paul meant when he called upon the people to "present your bodies a living sacrifice, holy, acceptable unto God"? (Romans 12:1). Isn't that what Amaleki had in mind when he beckoned the readers of the Book of Mormon to "come unto Christ, who is the Holy One of Israel, and partake of his salvation, and the power of his redemption. Yea, come unto him, and offer your whole souls as an offering unto him"? (Omni 1:26).

Because he is a living God, our Heavenly Father is forevermore involved in this matter of change. In the beginning he spoke, chaotic matter responded, and the heavens and the earth were formed. The placement of Adam and Eve and all forms of life on earth changed the nature of existence on this planet. Because of the fall of our first parents and because men and women are often enticed to wander from the strait and narrow path, the Father sent his Only Begotten Son to further alter the course of events on earth—to reverse what would otherwise continue as a movement toward dissolution. The Savior came into the world to change things, both cosmically and individually.

The gospel of Jesus Christ is all about change. True worship of the true and living God results in change. Betterment.

Improvement. More directly, it is about the transformation of the human soul by and through the redeeming mercy and atoning power of Jesus Christ. It is the miracle we know as spiritual rebirth, the manner in which we are made alive in Christ.

Underlying all that is said in this book are two propositions: first, that we too often tend to live beneath our spiritual privileges and to settle for twilight when sunlight is readily available; and second, that our God is ever ready to extend his remarkable blessings to us in a variety of ways and seeks to bring about a mighty change in us through several channels. In short, he who is omniscient and omnipotent is hardly limited to one avenue or course of action in our lives; spiritual change or conversion may take many forms. I am persuaded that one day, when we are able to review the divine movie of our own life and times, all of us will marvel at the truly mysterious ways and manner in which the omniloving One orchestrated the events and worked his wonders in our lives.

Christians always look for things all about us that turn our minds from worldliness to holiness, that remind us of Whose we are. For some the cross is a symbol and grand reminder of what it cost the Father to make salvation available to us. For some it is a CTR ring ("Choose the right") or a WWJD bracelet ("What would Jesus do?") that brings to remembrance the covenant we made at the time of baptism to keep his commandments, so that we might always have his Spirit to be with us (Moroni 4; 5). We need reminders, for we are summoned to go about doing good, just as Jesus did (Acts 10:38). Christ "suffered for us, leaving us an example, that [we] should follow his steps" (1 Peter 2:21). And so it is that the Prototype of saved beings beckons to us to be like him, to imitate his behavior, to emulate his matchless life.

"Come worship the Lord!" counseled Elder Bruce R. McConkie. "How is it done? Perfect worship is emulation. We honor those whom we imitate. The most perfect way of worship is to be holy as Jehovah is holy. It is to be pure as Christ is pure. It is to do the things that enable us to become like the Father."[5] Over time and as we begin to partake of the divine nature, we progress in our perspective of the Master from acknowledgment to astonishment to admiration to aspiration to adoration to affection. Through dedication and transformation, we move toward emulation, toward the imitation of the Christ. We begin to think and feel and act as he would. We will then be in that marvelous state of mind and heart in which, being purified as he is pure, we will see him as he is (1 John 3:1–3).

Chapter 10

OUR CLIMB TO HIGHER GROUND

You cannot lift another soul until you are standing on higher ground than he is," President Harold B. Lee stated. "You must be sure, if you would rescue the man, that you yourself are setting the example of what you would have him be. You cannot light a fire in another soul unless it is burning in your own soul."[1] The amount of good we can do in this world is largely a product of where we stand.

Life is a mission, not a career. We are not mortals seeking to have an occasional spiritual experience. Rather, we are spiritual and eternal beings having a brief mortal experience. We are here for a short time to "prepare to meet God" once again (Alma 34:32).

We live in a fallen condition, in a telestial world where we never really feel at home. Something deep down within us whispers that we are "stranger[s] here," that we have "wandered from a more exalted sphere,"[2] that our eternal journey has been punctuated by a temporary stay on earth. This divine homesickness will prompt us frequently to open our eyes to the beauties about us, to open our hearts to the sweet relationships we develop with family and friends, to open our minds to the lessons we can learn through joyous experiences and painful ones. That inner uneasiness will also remind us, again and again, that our success in life will not be determined by the abundance of the things that we possess (Luke 12:15) or the accolades and praise that might be heaped upon us. In this world our joy is not full (D&C 101:36). Our best days lie ahead.

In this life we are constantly provided with moments that matter. Often, these are sweet exchanges, but sometimes sour engagements test our mettle and show us what we are really made of. They demand a response from us, a response that will either contribute incrementally, bit by tiny bit, to the establishment of a Christlike character or transform us gradually into persons who live well beneath their spiritual privileges.

At one time or another, at some point in our lives, we must confront our day of decision and face some ever-present questions: Will I decide, once and for all, that I will live the law of the celestial kingdom, that I will "stay on the Lord's side of the line,"[3] that for me it will be "the Kingdom of God or nothing"?[4] Or will I, like ancient Israel, fluctuate "between two opinions" (1 Kings 18:21), vacillate between God's ways and the world's ways, compromise my covenants, dilute my discipleship, weaken my eternal resolve, and end up making the same decisions over and over again? Shall I decide now, once and for all, or shall I revisit this day of decision continually?

We were surrounded by holiness before we were born, and we need urgently to take time to be holy in this life: to search for good and wholesome and uplifting activities and to avoid like a plague—for that is exactly what they are—any and all things that damage, deter, degrade, desensitize, and place us on a detour from the path of righteousness. Holiness is wholeness. When we are holy, we are together, integrated, one, stable, undivided in our affections, at one in our desires, at peace in our hearts and minds. There is no noise within us. The great Jehovah issues the clarion call: "Be ye holy; for I am holy" (1 Peter 1:16; see also Leviticus 11:44). Indeed, the Holy One of Israel has called and commissioned us to "be a special people unto himself, above all people that are upon the face of the earth" (Deuteronomy 7:6). To do this, it has always been necessary for those seeking holiness to "put [a] difference between holy and unholy, and between unclean and clean" (Leviticus 10:10), to draw the line solidly in our minds between right and wrong and to stay on the proper side of that line.

People who are serious about spiritual things do not flirt with uncleanness, do not see how close they can get to the edge without quite going all the way. Too many who profess to be disciples of the Savior maintain such attitudes as the following: "I want to be good, I really do, but I don't want to be *too* good." Or, "I want to try my hand at sinning for a while, just a little, without getting my hands dirty." In other words, "I want to be bad, but not *too* bad." Such ritual prodigalism in which premeditated sinning and repentance characterize attitudes and behavior are offensive to God and off-putting to the Holy Spirit. Those who continue to fly near the flame will eventually be burned.

In a world that is spinning out of control, a world whose moral and ethical values are sinking toward Sodom and gliding toward Gomorrah, we cannot afford to look to the confused for counsel. We dare not turn to a secular society for solutions. And we certainly cannot allow ourselves to imitate or adopt the clothing styles, manner of speech, or forms of entertainment that the unclean and the ungodly have chosen. We must somehow demand and maintain a style of our own. As Latter-day Saints we must stand up, speak out, and voice our deepest concerns about the way things are headed. We can represent a new kind of countercultural influence; we can begin a righteous revolution, the kind of revolution that would please our Lord and Master and ease the burdens of the apostles and prophets charged to guide the destiny of his Church.

Isaiah the prophet wrote, "Who among us shall dwell with the devouring fire?" meaning, Who will dwell eventually with our Heavenly Father in celestial glory? He continues: "Who among us shall dwell with everlasting burnings?" Note the answer: "*He that walketh righteously, and speaketh uprightly*; he that despiseth the gain of oppressions, that shaketh his hands from holding of bribes, *that stoppeth his ears from hearing of blood, and shutteth his eyes from seeing evil; he shall dwell on high*" (Isaiah 33:14–16; italics added).

Of course we must be aware of the evils of our world; we must know what is out there in order to discern it and avoid it. But we need not obsess over these things; we need not spend our time focusing unduly on immorality or greed or crime. Rather, as the apostle Paul advised, "Whatsoever things are true, whatsoever things are honest, whatsoever things are just, whatsoever things are pure, whatsoever things are lovely, whatsoever things are of good report; if there be any virtue, and if there be any praise, *think on these things*" (Philippians 4:8; italics added; compare Articles of Faith 1:13).

Such divine counsel and direction will of necessity govern the television shows we watch and refuse to watch; the movies we attend or we bring into our homes; the music we permit to occupy the stage of our minds; and, yes, the quality of people with whom we associate each day. We must be especially cautious about efforts to rescue others from questionable places or compromising situations. If entering such an environment causes us to forfeit, even momentarily, the influence of the Spirit of God, we must think twice. Is the risk really worth it? Do we stand to lose more than we might gain? We must always go toward the light, for light will chase darkness from among us (D&C 50:25).

The Lord has instructed us that in order to keep ourselves unspotted from the world, we should "go to the house of prayer and offer up [our] sacraments upon [his] holy day; for verily this is a day appointed unto you to rest from your labors, and to pay thy devotions unto the Most High; nevertheless thy vows shall be offered up in righteousness on all days and at all times" (D&C 59:9–11). If we are serious about climbing to higher ground, we will be found in church every Sunday—attending all of our meetings, partaking of the sacrament, participating in Sunday School, and contributing to the spirit found in Relief Society, Primary, and priesthood meetings. The Lord needs us. He needs us to be knowledgeable, dependable, and competent disciples. We need to know not only that the gospel is true but we need to know the gospel, better than we do right now. We need to be in the right place at the right time. We will thereby become the right person.

Daily immersion in the holy scriptures exposes us consistently to holiness, to the mind and will and word of the Lord. When we feel the Holy Spirit that derives from our study of scripture, we hear the voice of the Lord to us (D&C 18:34–36), for "[his] voice is Spirit" (D&C 88:66). When we want to speak to God, we pray—morning, night, and all through the day in our hearts. When we want to hear God speak to us, we read the word of God. And if we are in tune, if we seek inspiration appropriately, "new writing" appears before us (1 Nephi 16:29). The scriptures thereby become timely as well as timeless, and they demonstrate their eternal relevance.

Now, above and beyond all that might be said, the greatest and most significant invitation we have received is simply to come unto Christ. He is the Vine, and we are the branches; without him we can do nothing (John 15:5). It is through Jesus Christ and his suffering and atoning sacrifice, in the garden of Gethsemane and on the cross of Calvary, that we can be forgiven of our sins, cleansed of pride and

arrogance and ego, purified of worldly wishing and telestial thinking, and granted divine grace or enabling power
to face and overcome temptations, carry out the otherwise
impossible, and cast Satan out of our lives. We "grow up
unto the Lord" (Helaman 3:21) into a life of holiness, happiness, and genuine fulfillment. Jesus Christ is not just our
last chance; he is, as Sister Sheri Dew pointed out, our *only*
chance.[5] Without him, without his tender mercies, without
his strength and goodness in our lives, we can do nothing
and ultimately are nothing.

To paraphrase C. S. Lewis, I believe in Christ as I believe
in the sun, not because I can see it, but because of it I can
see all other things so much more clearly.[6] Because he lives,
everything else comes to life. Because his mission of mercy is
in fact the fundamental principle of our religion,[7] everything
else about our religion makes sense and contributes to our
sanctification and ultimate salvation. Christ is the Center,
and without center, can there be circumference?

Elder Joseph B. Wirthlin observed: "After His Resurrection, the Savior came to the Americas. Because of His
wondrous ministry, the people's hearts were softened. They
abandoned their sins and journeyed to higher ground. They
cherished His words and sought to follow His example.

"They lived so righteously that there were no contentions
among them, and they dealt justly one with another. They
shared freely of their substance one with another, and they
prospered exceedingly.

"Of this people it was said that 'surely there could not be

a happier people among all the people who had been created by the hand of God' (4 Nephi 1:16).

"In our day we face a similar choice. We can foolishly ignore the prophets of God, depend on our own strength, and ultimately reap the consequences. Or, we can wisely draw near to the Lord and partake of His blessings. . . .

"This journey to higher ground is the pathway of discipleship to the Lord Jesus Christ. It is a journey that will ultimately lead us to exaltation with our families in the presence of the Father and the Son. Consequently, our journey to higher ground must include the house of the Lord. As we come unto Christ and journey to higher ground, we will desire to spend more time in His temples, because the temples represent higher ground, sacred ground.

"In every age we are faced with a choice. We can trust in our own strength, or we can journey to higher ground and come unto Christ.

"Each choice has a consequence.

"Each consequence, a destination."[8]

A significant aspect of worshipping our Lord is seeking to emulate him. There must be a righteous obsession on our part to have clean hands and a pure heart (Psalm 24:4), to live well above the norm, to strive for the serenity that comes only through self-denial and self-surrender, to look for the good and the beautiful and the praiseworthy in our world, and to be anxiously engaged in the climb to higher ground.

Chapter 11
THE OBJECT OF OUR WORSHIP

In his great Intercessory Prayer given following his Last Supper, Jesus pleaded with the Father to make his disciples one as they (the Father and the Son) were one. Earlier in this same prayer Jesus uttered the following timeless words, words that spell out our relationship with the Lord and what he expects of us: "And this is life eternal, that they might know thee the only true God, and Jesus Christ, whom thou hast sent" (John 17:3). This is a tremendously important message; whole books could be written on this specific verse. In the long run, it will matter precious little what we know about science or history or anthropology or literature or art if we have not come to know, through the power of the Holy Spirit, the God we worship. That is the great purpose of mortality and thus the quest of a lifetime.

St. Thomas Aquinas, the great Christian church philosopher and theologian, taught that in the long run we cannot really know what God is, only *what he is not*. Although I tend to disagree with Aquinas on this, especially in light of the passage in John—I've come over the years to appreciate that it may be just as important to know what the Lord is not as to know what he is. In that light, let's consider some things that the Lord Jesus Christ or our Heavenly Father is not.

1. *Neither the Father nor the Son is a cosmic errand boy.* I mean no disrespect or irreverence in so saying, but I do intend to convey the idea that while they love us deeply and dearly, the Father and the Son are not perched on the edge of heaven, anxiously anticipating our next wish. I doubt anyone would ever state that he or she considers the Lord to be our servant in any way; at the same time, we sometimes act as though we do believe that. For one thing, when we speak of God as being *good* to us, we generally mean that he is *kind* to us. In the words of the inimitable C. S. Lewis, "What would really satisfy us would be a god who said of anything we happened to like doing, 'What does it matter so long as they are contented?' We want, in fact, not so much a father in heaven as a grandfather in heaven—a senile benevolence who, as they say, 'liked to see young people enjoying themselves,' and whose plan for the universe was simply that it might be truly said at the end of each day, 'a good time was had by all.'"[1] You know and I know that God is much, much more than that.

That some of us may tend to view God as a servant is also evident in the way we pray. Let's ask ourselves a few questions: Are our prayers intended to be conversation or a lecture, a chat or a command? Do our prayers take the form of a monologue or a dialogue? Are our prayers dominated by an endless list of things we want done and done right away? How much time do we spend in prayers thanking God specifically for blessings, meaningful events in our lives, and maybe even (in looking back) a few of the trials that have worked to shape our personality and our character?

Our Lord is not just a force in the universe, not just a cosmic gas that somehow transforms chaos into meaning. Rather, God is a person. He has feelings, and although he does not need our love or our obedience in order to remain God, he knows that our greatest happiness in this life and in the life to come will result from coming to know him more surely each day.

One writer observed that "when we so emphasize Christ's benefits that he becomes nothing more than what his significance is 'for me,' we are in danger. . . . Evangelism [missionary work] that says 'come on, it's good for you'; discipleship that concentrates on the benefits package; sermons that 'use' Jesus as the means to a better life or marriage or job or attitude—these all turn Jesus into an expression of that nice god who always meets my spiritual needs. And this is why I am increasingly hesitant to speak of Jesus as my *personal* Lord and Savior. As Ken Woodward put it . . . , 'Now I think we all need to be converted—over and over again, but having a personal savior has always struck me as, well, elitist, like having a personal tailor. I'm satisfied to have the same Lord and Savior as everyone else.' Jesus is not a personal Savior who only seeks to meet my needs. He is the risen, crucified Lord of all creation who seeks to guide me back into the truth."[2]

How we view God is critical. As in most areas of our existence, balance is vital. On the one hand, God is God: he is omnipotent (all powerful), omniscient (all knowing), and, by means of his Holy Spirit, omnipresent (everywhere present). At the same time, as Enoch learned so poignantly, he is there when we need him (Moses 7:30). His infinity does not preclude either his immediacy or his intimacy. One Christian writer stated, "I want neither a terrorist spirituality that keeps me in a perpetual state of fright about being in right relationship with my heavenly Father nor a sappy spirituality that portrays God as such a benign teddy bear that there is no aberrant behavior or desire of mine that he will not condone."[3]

2. *Jesus was not just a Galilean guru nor was he a Samaritan Socrates.* It is fascinating to read the New Testament Gospels looking specifically for such things as what Jesus said, how he said it, how he responded to questions, and how he dealt with criticism and ridicule. To be sure, Jesus Christ was one bright man. He seemed to always have the right answer for the right situation. But he was more than a teacher, more than an inspiring teacher, more than a great moral teacher. He was the Son of God, God the Son. That means he was more than a composite of intelligent answers, more than walking wisdom. In him was understanding and insight, but, more important, inside him were the powers of godliness, the powers of immortality.

I've traveled a good deal and met many persons of other

faiths throughout the world and also many extremely bright and notable personalities who claim to have no faith at all. When the conversation turns to the person and powers of Jesus of Nazareth, too often I hear what has become almost a laughable declaration: "I think Jesus was an extremely intelligent man, a great peacemaker, and a dispenser of gems of wisdom. But I do not believe he was God."

In response to that assertion, let me quote C. S. Lewis: "A man who is merely a man and said the sort of things Jesus said would not be a great moral teacher. He would either be a lunatic—on a level with the man who says he is a poached egg—or else he would be the Devil of Hell. You must make your choice. Either this man was, and is, the Son of God: or else a madman or something worse. You can shut Him up for a fool, you can spit at Him and kill Him as a demon; or you can fall at His feet and call him Lord and God. But let us not come with any patronising nonsense about His being a great human teacher. He has not left that open to us. He did not intend to."[4] Further, "If Christianity only means one more bit of good advice, then Christianity is of no importance. There has been no lack of good advice for the last four thousand years. A bit more makes no difference."[5]

3. *The Lord is not "religious."* Now before you take this book and throw it out the window or into the fireplace, let me explain what I mean. The Latin word *religio* originally meant a binding obligation, a rather special obligation. In that sense, religion represents the effort of humankind to apply true principles and doctrines in order to enable mortals

to keep their obligation, their covenants with the Almighty. You may recognize in the word *religion* the root of another word that you also know well—the word *ligament*. A ligament is a fibrous tissue that binds or links bone to cartilage or that holds organs in place. Thus the true purpose of God-ordained religion is to link or tie mortal humans to an immortal, exalted Deity. As the apostle James taught, "Pure religion and undefiled before God and the Father is this, To visit the fatherless and widows in their affliction, and to keep himself unspotted from the vices of the world" (JST, James 1:27).

In other words, pure religion deals with two main aspects of our lives: how we treat other people and to what extent we strive to remain free from sin in a sinful world. Obviously, in this sense God is religious.

Too often, however, as C. S. Lewis pointed out, religion has been separated from everyday life and made into just another aspect or dimension of our lives.[6] Thus we speak of our intellectual life, our athletic life, our social life, and our religious life. Religion is reduced to being one of the pieces of the larger pie. "Authentic Christianity," beloved Christian writer Brennan Manning observed, is not "a code of dos and don'ts, not a tedious moralizing, not a list of forbidding commandments, and certainly not the necessary minimum requirement for avoiding the pains of hell. Life in the Spirit," he continues, "is the thrill and the excitement of being loved by and falling in love with Jesus Christ."[7]

True religion represents something much, much deeper. It

is our link with God, our tie to the Infinite, and thus should and must inform and affect every other phase of our existence. Religion isn't something we do on Sunday and then go about our business the other six days of the week. As Latter-day Saints, our religion is more than religion; it is life, a 24/7 life.

Several years ago, when I was teaching the Gospel Doctrine class in our ward, my wife Shauna and I were trying to decide whether we should go to a particular movie one Saturday evening. We had heard that it was quite good, but we also knew that it was rated PG-13 and that there were some objectionable parts. I finally said to Shauna: "Let's don't go. I have to teach Sunday School in the morning, and I don't want to do anything that would mess up my mind and keep me from enjoying the Spirit of the Lord." And so we talked and read for a few hours that night.

As I laid my head on the pillow about 11:00 P.M., I reflected on what a noble choice I had made, on how wonderful it was that I had exercised the appropriate restraint. And then there came the unanticipated thought: "So you think you're really something, huh? Well, what if this had been a Tuesday night or a Thursday night? Would you still have been as concerned about tarnishing your mind and heart? Would you have gone to the movie then, or do you plan to go next Wednesday or Friday?"

My smug self-righteousness was rapidly transformed into the remorseful realization that ours is a seven-days-a-week religion and I should be just as concerned about what I consume on Monday morning as I am on Saturday night. My vows, meaning my covenants, made at baptism and in the holy temple, should and must guide me throughout the entire week (D&C 59:11).

A final thought about religion. People, even strongly religious people, need to guard against the tendency for their religion to become ritualized. One great challenge we face as a Church is a happy challenge—the challenge of Church growth. Not only does that mean we have to prepare more and more young people to serve full-time missions and more new converts to serve as leaders, we must also see to it that we do not allow ourselves to be directed solely by rules and written regulations. This is the Lord's Church, and he is at the head. Because it is his Church, it is to be conducted according to his plan and under his direction, through the Holy Spirit. If we become too rigid, we risk losing that marvelous spiritual spontaneity that has characterized Latter-day Saints since the days of Joseph Smith. Pure religion involves what we do as well as *who and what we are and what we are becoming*. Pure religion is a thing of both the heart and the head.

4. *Jesus is not just my Elder Brother.* Latter-day Saints have insight into our eternal existence that persons of other faiths do not have. For example, we view many of the things that happen to us in this life, including traumas and tragedies, with a more elevated perspective, given what we know about our having lived as spirits before we were born into mortality. In our first estate, our premortal existence, we were taught, trained, and prepared to come to earth and take on

a wondrous mortal body, all as a very significant part of the overall plan of salvation. John the Beloved opened his magnificent Gospel with this statement: "In the beginning was the Word, and the Word was with God, and the Word was God. The same was in the beginning with God. All things were made by him; and without him was not any thing made that was made" (John 1:1–3). That is, in the premortal life Christ, here designated as the Word, was with our Heavenly Father. In fact, Christ was God in that first estate. As God and leader of the "noble and great ones" (Abraham 3:22; 4:1), he created worlds without number (Moses 1:33; 7:30). It is appropriate, therefore, that we refer to Jesus Christ as our Elder Brother as pertaining to the premortal life.

It is of great interest to me, however, that of the almost one hundred names given to our Lord and Savior by the Nephite prophets, the term "Elder Brother" is never used once. He is called the Almighty, the Almighty God, Alpha and Omega, Creator, Eternal Father, Eternal God, Eternal Head, Eternal Judge, Everlasting God, Father of heaven and of earth, God, God of Abraham, God of nature, Holy Messiah, Holy One of Israel, Immanuel, Keeper of the gate, Lamb of God, Lord God Almighty, Lord God Omnipotent, Lord God of hosts, Mighty One of Israel, Most High God, Redeemer of Israel, Supreme Being, True and Living God, True Messiah, but never "Elder Brother." In other words, I'm convinced that because the Nephites looked upon Christ with such awe and viewed him with such majesty, it did not occur to them to refer to him as Elder Brother. He was God.

Elder M. Russell Ballard explained: "We occasionally hear some members refer to Jesus as our Elder Brother, which is a true concept based on our understanding of the premortal life with our Father in Heaven. But like many points of gospel doctrine, that simple truth doesn't go far enough in terms of describing the Savior's role in our present lives and His great position as a member of the Godhead. Thus, some non-LDS Christians are uncomfortable with what they perceive as a secondary role for Christ in our theology. They feel that we view Jesus as a spiritual peer. They believe that we view Christ as an implementer for God, if you will, but that we don't view Him as God to us and to all mankind, which, of course, is counter to biblical testimony about Christ's divinity.

"Let me help us understand, with clarity and testimony, our belief about Jesus Christ. We declare He is the King of Kings, Lord of Lords, the Creator, the Savior, the Captain of our Salvation, the Bright and Morning Star. He has taught us that He is in all things, above all things, through all things and round about all things, that He is Alpha and Omega, the Lord of the Universe, the first and the last relative to our salvation, and that His name is above every name and is in fact the only name under heaven by which we can be saved. . . .

"[W]e can understand why some Latter-day Saints have tended to focus on Christ's Sonship as opposed to His Godhood. As members of earthly families, we can relate to Him as a child, as a Son, and as a Brother because we know how that feels. We can personalize that relationship because we ourselves are children, sons and daughters, brothers and sisters. For some it may be more difficult to relate to Him as a God. And so in an attempt to draw closer to Christ and to cultivate warm and personal feelings toward Him, some tend to humanize Him, sometimes at the expense of acknowledging His Divinity. So let us be very clear on this point: it is true that Jesus was our Elder Brother in the premortal life, but we believe that in this life it is crucial that we become 'born again' as His sons and daughters in the gospel covenant."[8]

5. *Christ is not our buddy.* There's a natural tendency, and it is a dangerous one, to seek to bring Jesus down to our level in an effort to draw closer to him. This is a problem among people both in and outside the LDS faith. Of course we should seek with all our hearts to draw near to him. Of course we should strive to set aside all barriers that would prevent us from closer fellowship with him. And of course we should pray and labor and serve in an effort to close the gap between what we are and what we should be. But drawing close to the Lord is serious business; spirituality is something to be worked at, not played with.

There are a number of gospel ironies in the scriptures. One of them is the irony that only those who lose their lives in service to the Lord find their life   eternal life (Matthew 16:25–26). Jesus said on one occasion that he came to bring not peace but a sword, "to set a man at variance against his father, and the daughter against her mother . . . and a man's foes shall be they of his own household" (Matthew 10:34–36).

How odd! Jesus is the Prince of Peace, and everyone knows that he above all would want family members to be close, to be united. He is teaching here, however, that sometimes the price of receiving and living the gospel is a price that may indeed separate you from those you love.

Another gospel irony is that the way to get close to the Lord is not by attempting in any way to shrink the distance between us and him, to emphasize his humanity rather than his divinity, or to speak to him or of him in casual language. In fact, as King Benjamin explained, you and I are enabled to obtain a remission of sins from day to day by recognizing Christ's magnificence, his majesty, his power, and the truth that without him we are unprofitable servants who are less than the dust of the earth (Mosiah 2:20–25; 4:11–12).

Perhaps the greatest lesson that the mighty lawgiver Moses learned was a lesson that followed a transcendent encounter with Deity and a panoramic vision of God's creations: "And it came to pass that it was for the space of many hours before Moses did again receive his natural strength like unto man; and he said unto himself: Now, *for this cause I know that man is nothing,* which thing I never had supposed" (Moses 1:10; italics added). It has been my experience that on the whole Latter-day Saints do not do "awe" very well. By that I mean we are less inclined than some of our friends of other faiths to be staggered and sobered by God's omnipotence, omniscience, and omnipresence.

The scriptures teach that our God is a consuming fire (Hebrews 12:29). One commentator pointed out: "This is no Christ the humanitarian, Christ the master of interpersonal relationships, or Christ the buddy. It is Christ the Lord and Savior who calls us to repent, change our lives, and strike out in a new direction."[9] Those who have come to know the Lord best—the prophets, or covenant spokesmen—are also those who speak of him in reverent tones, who, like Isaiah, find themselves crying out, "Woe is me! for I am undone; because I am a man of unclean lips, and I dwell in the midst of a people of unclean lips: for mine eyes have seen the King, the Lord of hosts" (Isaiah 6:5). Coming into the presence of the Almighty is no light thing; we respond soberly to God's command to Moses: "Put off thy shoes from off thy feet, for the place whereon thou standest is holy ground" (Exodus 3:5).

This is a terribly difficult balance to strike. "I fully agree," observed C. S. Lewis, "that the relationship between God and a man is more private and intimate than any possible relationship between two fellow creatures. Yes, but at the same time there is, in another way, a greater distance between the participants. . . . We ought to be—sometimes I hope one is—simultaneously aware of closest proximity and infinite distance."[10]

6. *Jesus Christ is not just the "God of the gaps."* Several years ago fellow religion professor Stephen Robinson and I were invited to Kansas City to spend a day in conversation with leaders of the Southern Baptist Convention. We talked

together for about seven hours that day. At a certain point in the conversation, however, one of our Baptist friends made the comment, "But of course you folks do not believe in the grace of Jesus Christ." Steve and I both leaned forward in our chairs to try to convince our new acquaintances that in fact we did believe in and teach the importance of salvation by the grace of Christ.

One of our friend's associates responded: "Yes, we understand—you believe in the God of the gaps."

I replied, "I've never heard that before in my life. Who or what is the God of the gaps?"

He explained that he understood that Latter-day Saints believed in a kind of works-righteousness, that individuals are to do everything they can in expending all of their efforts and then Jesus would fill in the remaining deficit.

An hour later, after seeking again and again to dissuade them from their caricature of Mormonism, Steve and I realized that we had failed.

Of course Jesus Christ, the One who makes all the difference in our salvation, will make up the difference at the time of judgment, at least for those who have come to trust in and rely upon him. But too often I fear that Latter-day Saints think that we are expected to do our 85 or 90 percent and leave the remainder, a small percentage, for Jesus to handle. That is incorrect and misleading, inasmuch as it causes us to overstate our own role in salvation and grossly understate the role of him who has bought us with his blood. The scripture that seems to lend itself to this misunderstanding, is, oddly enough, 2 Nephi 25:23: "For we labor diligently to write, to persuade our children, and also our brethren, to believe in Christ, and to be reconciled to God; for we know that it is by grace that we are saved, after all we can do."

I have met members throughout the Church who suppose that this means Christ can help us on the day of judgment only *after* we have expended our best efforts and done everything we know how to do. Who do you know that will have done *everything* they could have done? Who do you know who will have spent every waking hour of every day of every year serving God tirelessly and tenaciously? Only one person fits this bill, and that was the Lord Jesus Christ himself; he was the only one to live a perfectly sinless life. Further, I sincerely believe that what Nephi is trying to teach is that we are saved by the grace of Jesus Christ—his unmerited divine favor, his unearned divine assistance, his enabling power—*above and beyond* all we can do, *notwithstanding* all we can do, *in spite of* all we can do—which will never be enough.

Too often we're inclined to think of grace as the Lord's final boost into celestial glory hereafter. To be sure, we will need all the divine help we can get in order to qualify to go where God and angels are. But the grace of God is extended to you and me every hour of every day and is not limited to the bar of judgment.

Let me say this another way. If there had been no atonement of Christ, no amount of good works on our part could ever, worlds without end, make up for its absence. "No matter how hard we work," Elder Ballard has pointed out, "no matter how much we obey, no matter how many good things we do in this life, it would not be enough were it not for Jesus Christ and His loving grace. On our own we cannot earn the kingdom of God—no matter what we do. Unfortunately, there are some within the Church who have become so preoccupied with performing good works that they forget that those works—as good as they may be—are hollow unless they are accompanied by a complete dependence on Christ."[11]

Jesus is central to the plan of salvation; he is vital and indispensable. We cannot save ourselves. We cannot earn our exaltation. We cannot exercise sufficient grit and willpower to do the works of righteousness and battle against Satan on our own. Christ is our Lord, our Savior, our Redeemer, and our King. He is the Lord of Hosts, meaning the Lord of Armies, the Captain of our Salvation. He is God, and if it were not so, he could not save us. He is the God we worship. Without him, we have nothing. With him, we have everything.

Chapter 12

STRIVING AND STEADY

I n our quest to worship the Lord Jesus Christ in spirit and in truth, we find it a significant challenge to navigate the strait and narrow path in a stable and consistent manner, to work with zeal and with patient maturity, to stay in the mainstream of the Church. God does not expect us to work ourselves into spiritual, emotional, or physical exhaustion, nor does he desire that we be truer than true. There is little virtue in excess, even in gospel excess. In fact, as persons exceed the bounds of propriety and go beyond the established mark, they open themselves to deception and ultimately to destruction. Imbalance leads to instability. If Satan cannot entice us to sins of commission, it just may be that he will cause our strength—our zeal for goodness and righteousness—to become our weakness. He will encourage excess, for any virtue, when taken to the extreme, becomes a vice.

For one thing, persons who determine upon a course that will take them beyond the expected, above the required, inevitably begin to expect the same of others. It becomes a "religious" principle to which associates are proselyted. The overzealous tend to judge others by their own standard. I have known persons who are so completely committed to family history and temple work that they badger and criticize others who are not doing as much as they are. Obviously such work is a vital part of our ministry as Latter-day Saints; we neglect it at the peril of our eternal salvation. I also know, as Elder Dallin H. Oaks has pointed out, that there is a time and a season for all things, that individuals' specific contributions to the kingdom are and must be private consecrations. That is why the leaders of the Church have discouraged quotas for temple work. "Our efforts to promote temple and family history work," Elder Oaks observed, "should be such as to accomplish the work of the Lord, not to impose guilt on his children. Members of this church have many individual circumstances—age, health, education, place of residence, family responsibilities, financial circumstances, accessibility to sources for individual or library research, and many others. If we encourage members in this work without taking these individual circumstances into account, we may do more to impose guilt than to further the work. . . . There are many different things our members can do to help in the redeeming of the dead, in temple and family history work. Some involve callings. Others are personal. All are expressions of devotion and discipleship. All present opportunities for sacrifice and service."[1]

I spoke once to a temple president who described what had happened over the years in the temple in which he and his wife had served. He said that a particular room was set aside as a prayer room, a place where patrons of the temple could retire for pondering and meditation, where they could go to seek inspiration or guidance on personal matters. For the longest time, he said, the room served a useful purpose: it reminded the patrons that temples were places of learning and revelation, holy edifices where we go to attend to sacred matters for the living as well as the dead. In time, however, the room became such a popular spot that long lines were often seen winding their way around the celestial room, as hosts of people stood waiting for their turn. "Brother Millet," the president observed, "sometimes people went into the room, and we simply couldn't get them out. Some of them," he added, "would pray themselves into a frenzy."

The tendency to take a good thing and run it into the ground has been called a "gospel hobby." Gospel hobbies lead to imbalance. To instability. To distraction. To misperception. They are dangerous and should be avoided as we would any other sin. President Joseph F. Smith said: "We frequently look about us and see people who incline to extremes, who are fanatical. We may be sure that this class of people do not understand the gospel. They have forgotten, if they ever knew, that it is very unwise to take a fragment of truth and treat it as if it were the whole thing."[2]

On another occasion President Smith taught: "Brethren and sisters, don't have hobbies. Hobbies are dangerous in the Church of Christ. They are dangerous because they give undue prominence to certain principles or ideas to the detriment and dwarfing of others just as important, just as binding, just as saving as the favored doctrines or commandments.

"Hobbies give to those who encourage them a false aspect of the gospel of the Redeemer; they distort and place out of harmony its principles and teachings. The point of view is unnatural. Every principle and practice revealed from God is essential to man's salvation, and to place any one of them unduly in front, hiding and dimming all others, is unwise and dangerous; it jeopardizes our salvation, for it darkens our minds and beclouds our understandings. . . .

"We have noticed this difficulty: that Saints with hobbies are prone to judge and condemn their brethren and sisters who are not so zealous in the one particular direction of their pet theory as they are. . . . There is another phase of this difficulty—the man with a hobby is apt to assume an 'I am holier than thou' position, to feel puffed up and conceited, and to look with distrust, if with no severer feeling, on his brethren and sisters who do not so perfectly live that one particular law."[3]

In other words, an emphasis upon excellence in gospel living—as manifested in gospel hobbies—can result in pride, the father of all other sins. President Harold B. Lee explained that at times "people who pride themselves on their strict observance of the rules and ordinances and ceremonies of the Church are led astray by false spirits, who exercise an influence so imitative of that which proceeds from a Divine source that even these persons, who think they are 'the very elect,' find it difficult to discern the essential difference."⁴

True excellence in gospel living—compliance with established laws and ordinances in a quiet and patient manner—results in humility, in greater reliance upon God and a broadening love and acceptance of one's fellow man. What we are doing in the name of goodness ought to bring us closer to those we love and serve, ought to turn our hearts toward people, rather than cause us to turn up our noses in judgmental scorn and rejection. The greatest man to walk the earth, the only perfect human being, looked with tenderness and compassion upon those who, like most of us, tried hard but fell short.

Elder Bruce R. McConkie wrote: "It is . . . my experience that people who ride gospel hobbies, who try to qualify themselves as experts in some specialized field, who try to make the whole plan of salvation revolve around some field of particular interest to them—it is my experience that such persons are usually spiritually immature and spiritually unstable. This includes those who devote themselves—as though by divine appointment—to setting forth the signs of the times; or, to expounding about the Second Coming; or, to a faddist interpretation of the Word of Wisdom; or, to a twisted emphasis on temple work or any other doctrine or practice. The Jews of Jesus' day made themselves hobbyists and extremists in the field of Sabbath observance, and it colored and blackened their whole way of worship. We would do well to have a *sane, rounded, and balanced approach to the whole gospel and all of its doctrines.*"[5]

Not unrelated to excessive zeal and overmuch righteousness is the tendency by some to attempt to force spiritual things. What would we think of a father who said to his fourteen-year-old son: "Larry, if you really love me, you will be tall. I have been short all my life. I love basketball and have always wanted to be a star forward on a successful team. But it's never worked out. If you love me, if you have any respect for me as your father, you will grow to be six foot eight." Such a request would be cruel and unkind, especially given that Larry has little control over how tall he will be. He can eat the right foods, discipline his mind and body, and do everything within his power to become big and strong, but he cannot control how tall he will be.

In a way, it's the same with spiritual growth. We cannot program it. We cannot specify and delineate and produce. We cannot prepare formulas and plans that will result in specific spiritual phenomena. We cannot say with certitude that if we do X and Y and Z that a dream or vision will be forthcoming; or that if we do A or B or C consistently, we will be able to prophesy or speak in tongues. We can prepare the soil, so to speak; we can provide a setting for development, but that is all. We must exercise patience and trust in the Lord and his purposes.

President Boyd K. Packer has warned: "Such words as

compel, coerce, constrain, pressure, demand do not describe our privileges with the Spirit.

"You can no more force the Spirit to respond than you can force a bean to sprout, or an egg to hatch before its time. You can create a climate to foster growth; you can nourish, and protect; but you cannot force or compel: You must await the growth.

"Do not be impatient to gain great spiritual knowledge. Let it grow, help it grow; but do not force it, or you will open the way to be misled."[6]

Like the small oil lamps of the Middle East, which require a careful and methodical effort to fill, so in our own lives we need to build our reservoirs of faith and spiritual experience gradually and consistently. Consistent gospel growth—that is the answer. A colleague of mine drew my attention to these words of President Spencer W. Kimball: "The foolish [virgins] asked the others to share their oil, but spiritual preparedness cannot be shared in an instant. . . . This was not selfishness or unkindness. The kind of oil that is needed to illuminate the way and light up the darkness is not shareable. . . . In our lives the oil of preparedness is accumulated drop by drop in righteous living."[7]

In our eagerness to prepare and do all that is asked of us, we must be careful that our personal expectations, though rigorous, are realistic. Zion of old became a society of the pure in heart "in process of time" (Moses 7:21), and members of the Church become holy in similar fashion. Except for a small number of cases that are so miraculous they are written up in scripture, being born again is a process. Most often we are born again gradually, from one level of spiritual grace to a higher. Almost always we are sanctified—made clean and holy and pure through the blood of Christ by the medium of the Spirit—in gradual, line-upon-line fashion. Ultimate perfection and salvation are processes.

The scriptures set forth certain principles which, if we are sensitive to their implications, will keep us on course and thus assist us in our quest for holiness. In his response to Satan's temptation to use divine powers for personal gain, the Savior answered, "It is written, Man shall not live by bread alone, but by every word that proceedeth out of the mouth of God" (Matthew 4:4; compare D&C 84:44).

Every word. Not every other word, not those words that are most acceptable and pleasing, not those words that support my own peculiar predispositions or fascinations. *Every* word. Members of the Church would seldom become embroiled in doctrinal disputes, controversial dialogues, or gospel hobbies if they truly sought to live by *every word* that has come from the Lord, the scriptures, the prophets. To live by every word of God also implies the need to read and study widely, to seek for at least as much breadth in our gospel scholarship as we have depth, to seek to have the big picture. It has been wisely said that the greatest commentary on scripture is scripture.

The resurrected Lord delivered to his American Hebrews the doctrine of Christ, the need for all men and women to have faith, repent, be reborn, and to endure faithfully to the end. He then declared: "Verily, verily, I say unto you, that this is my doctrine, and whoso buildeth upon this buildeth upon my rock, and the gates of hell shall not prevail against them. And *whoso shall declare more or less than this, and establish it for my doctrine, the same cometh of evil,* and is not built upon my rock; but he buildeth upon a sandy foundation, and the gates of hell stand open to receive such when the floods come and the winds beat upon them" (3 Nephi 11:39–40; italics added).

In a modern revelation, the Lord spoke of bringing forth the Book of Mormon, another testament of Jesus Christ, in order that he might establish his gospel and alleviate contention and disputation: "Behold, this is my doctrine—whosoever repenteth and cometh unto me, the same is my church. *Whosoever declareth more or less than this, the same is not of me, but is against me;* therefore he is not of my church" (D&C 10:67–68; italics added). We need to live the gospel in such a way that we seek neither to add to nor take away from that which comes by and through the appointed channels of revelation for the Church.

The Book of Mormon prophet Jacob indicted the ancient Jews: "The Jews were a stiffnecked people; and *they despised the words of plainness,* and killed the prophets, and *sought for things that they could not understand.* Wherefore, because of their blindness, which *blindness came by looking beyond the mark,* they must needs fall; for God hath taken away his plainness from them, and delivered unto them many things which they cannot understand, because they desired it. And because they desired it God hath done it, that they may stumble" (Jacob 4:14; italics added).

What a fascinating situation! A people despised, or perhaps spurned or underappreciated, the words of plainness. They sought for things they could not understand, perhaps meaning they pushed themselves well beyond what had been revealed and thus beyond what they could appropriately grasp. They became blind by "looking beyond the mark." That is, they missed the point! They missed the main message! In the case of the Jews, they looked beyond the mark when Christ was the mark. They focused on the minutiae of commentary concerning the Law, when Christ was the message of the Law. They confused means with ends, tokens with covenants, ritual with religion.

Elder Dean L. Larsen offered the following insights into this unusual scriptural passage: "Jacob speaks of people who placed themselves in serious jeopardy in spiritual things because they were unwilling to accept simple, basic principles of truth. They entertained and intrigued themselves with 'things that they could not understand' (Jacob 4:14). They were apparently afflicted with a pseudosophistication and a snobbishness that gave them a false sense of superiority over those who came among them with the Lord's words of plainness. They went beyond the mark of wisdom and prudence and obviously failed to stay within the circle of fundamental gospel truths which provide a basis for faith. They must have reveled in speculative and theoretical matters that obscured for them the fundamental spiritual truths."[8]

We begin the process of spiritual maturity as we learn to treasure up the word of the Lord, a sure means of avoiding deception (Joseph Smith–Matthew 1:37); as we find satisfaction and great delight in poring over the fundamental doctrines of the gospel and discussing them; and as we wait upon the Lord to make us into new creatures and to reveal his purposes, all in his own time, and in his own way, and according to his own will (D&C 88:67–68). We yearn to be worthy of the transcendent promises made to those who "continue in the faith grounded and settled, and [are] not moved from the hope of the gospel" (Colossians 1:23).

Chapter 13
TRUSTING CHRIST

In the fall of the year, at the time of the Feast of Tabernacles and six months before our Lord would suffer and die for our sins and three days later be raised from the dead, a remarkable event occurred. Matthew records that some six days after Peter had borne a powerful witness of the Savior at Caesarea Philippi—"Thou art the Christ, the Son of the living God" (Matthew 16:16)—Jesus took Peter, James, and John into a high mountain and there was transfigured before them. Moses and Elijah appeared. Latter-day Saints believe, of course, that these ancient prophets, and perhaps others, delivered to the apostolic presidency the keys of the kingdom of God, as had been predicted by Jesus a week earlier.

Matthew goes on to describe a scene that unfolded when the Master descended from the mountain with his chief apostles. A man knelt at Jesus' feet and pleaded earnestly that the Savior heal his son, who was vexed with an evil spirit. "I brought him to thy disciples," the man reported, "and they could not cure him." Jesus rebuked and cast out the devil and then kindly chastened his disciples for their lack of faith, a faith that in this case required the aid of fasting and prayer (Matthew 17:14–21).

Mark adds a detail to this story that is precious and poignant. After the father had made his heartfelt request of the Lord, Jesus said, "If thou canst believe, all things are possible to him that believeth." Then comes this priceless verse, one that touches the chords of my heart: "And straightway the father of the child cried out, and said with tears, *Lord, I believe; help thou mine unbelief*" (Mark 9:23–24; italics added). What a magnificent revelation of this man's soul! What an insight into his sincerity, honesty, and transparency. Do his words not reverberate in your mind and heart? Do they not echo your own yearnings?

I have often wondered how I would respond if Christ were to appear to me and ask, "Do you have the faith to move that mountain to the lake to the north?" or "Do you understand the gospel well enough to teach the heads of nations and the intellectual elite of the world?" or "Is your life in order sufficient for you to work mighty miracles?" or even, "Can I depend upon you to be true and faithful to your covenants all the days of your life?"

Those are tough questions, and only a foolish or arrogant person would answer quickly in the affirmative. Most of us would respond much as did the father of the troubled child, "Lord, I can do anything you ask me to do, if you will stand

by me and assist me; I cannot do such a thing on my own."
That honest recognition, that elevated acknowledgment, is
vital. We really cannot "handle it" on our own; no person
who walks this earth is bright enough or disciplined enough
or spiritually mature enough to undertake such otherwise
impossible tasks without heaven's help.

While such feelings of appropriate inadequacy send us
regularly to our knees in humble surrender, they also bring to
us a quiet peace and a soothing rest, one that takes from our
shoulders the unwarranted weight of attempting to save ourselves. That is what the apostle Paul meant when he wrote,
"Therefore *being justified by faith, we have peace with God
through our Lord Jesus Christ:* by whom also we have access
by faith into this grace wherein we stand, and rejoice in hope
of the glory of God" (Romans 5:1–2; italics added). That is,
once we know that we are justified by our Lord and Savior—
made right with God, pronounced innocent, exonerated, forgiven, and empowered—and learn to lean on and rely upon
his mighty arm, then the frets and cares and worries and ob-
sessions associated with doubling and tripling our efforts and
working ourselves into frenzied exhaustion—these burdens
begin to dissipate and eventually disappear. In short, faith
in Christ brings peace. Faith in Christ brings rest. Faith in
Christ brings contentment and true fulfillment.

To have faith in Christ is to *believe* in him, and, as
Stephen Robinson pointed out beautifully in his book
Believing Christ (Deseret Book, 1992), it is to believe what the
Lord says. It is to believe that he really does love us, one and

all. To believe that he really can forgive our sins and clean our slate. To believe that he can purify and renew our nature. To believe that he can make us into people of purpose and power, people prepared to stand in holy places in this life and inherit the highest heaven in the life to come. To believe that because he rose from the dead, each and every one of us will one day do the same. To believe, in other words, that Jesus the Christ is in fact and in very deed all that he and his apostles and prophets have said he is. In other words, to have faith in Christ is to have complete *confidence* in him. "Believe in God," Benjamin counseled; "believe that he is, and that he created all things, both in heaven and in earth; believe that he has all wisdom, and all power, both in heaven and in earth; believe that man doth not comprehend all the things which the Lord can comprehend" (Mosiah 4:9).

To have faith in Christ is to *rely* wholly upon him (2 Nephi 31:19; Moroni 6:4)—to lean upon him in times of crisis, to draw strength from him in times of weakness, to receive peace from him in moments of tragedy, to repose oneself in his person and his powers. It has wisely been said that grace is God's acceptance of us, while *faith is our acceptance of God's acceptance of us*. In a sense, faith and *hope* seem to be two sides of the same coin. Hope in Christ always flows from faith in Christ and represents anticipation, expectation, and assurance that through our acceptance of the terms and conditions of the gospel covenant, we will gain everlasting life, eternal life, God's life (Moroni 7:40–42).

To have faith in Christ is to *trust* him. Think about that

for a minute. Why do I trust my friends Robert Matthews or Larry Dahl or Camille Fronk Olson or Joseph McConkie or Brent Top or Andy Skinner when it comes to doctrinal understanding? Because I know these people, love and admire them, have spent countless hours in fruitful discussion with them, and know what a price they have paid in their lives to be able to understand the gospel. Why do I trust my cardiologist? Because he has worked with hundreds of people with problems similar to mine and because I have come to know him, have come to know that he wants to keep me alive, have come to admire his abilities and his judgment. Why do I trust Shauna, my wife and best friend? Because we entered into sacred covenants together, committed ourselves to an eternal union, loved and reared our children, served each other and sacrificed for each other, dealt with pain and anguish and frustration together, and have spent much time together in prayer and in the temple. We love and trust each other.

I have come to trust Jesus Christ because I have come to know by sweet and painful experience that his timetable is far wiser than mine. When I want something, I want it now. I don't want to wait a week or a month or a year; I want it today! But my divine Redeemer knows the end from the beginning, and thus he knows what is best for me and what is not, when or whether I should pursue a certain path. I suppose that like Alma I sin in my wishes whenever I try to be someone the Lord does not want me to be. I should be content with what I have been called or assigned to do (Alma 29:3).

Let's get practical. Would any one of us really like to be a multimillionaire if that was not something the Lord wanted for us? Would we plot or push to get a promotion or a professional position if we knew that God had other plans for us? Would we aspire to some church calling if God wanted us to serve in the kingdom elsewhere? I would hope not. Trusting does not mean having no goals or ambition, exercising no discipline or determination. It does mean that we learn to yield our hearts to God (Helaman 3:35), that we seek to gain an eye single to the glory of God (D&C 88:67), that we acknowledge his omniscience and eternal perspective.

It is not uncommon to hear Latter-day Saints and persons of other faiths speak of the need to acknowledge the hand of the Lord in everything. In modern revelation God instructs us to "thank the Lord thy God in all things" and says further, "in nothing doth man offend God, or against none is his wrath kindled, save those who confess not his hand in all things, and obey not his commandments" (D&C 59:7, 21). Expressing gratitude is particularly easy to do when God has granted us something we wanted, something we have longed and prayed for, something that thrills us—making the team, getting the new job, the pay raise, the child we had hoped for, the acceptance notice to the university we have our heart set on attending. But how easy is it to thank God for the trying times, the challenging moments, the heartbreaking events? The Roman Catholic contemplative Henri Nouwen spoke of gratitude as follows:

"To be grateful for the good things that happen in our

lives is easy, but to be grateful for all of our lives—the good as well as the bad, the moments of joy as well as the moments of sorrow, the successes as well as the failures, the rewards as well as the rejections—that requires hard spiritual work. Still, we are only truly grateful people when we can say thank you to all that has brought us to the present moment. As long as we keep dividing our lives between events and people we would like to remember and those we would rather forget, we cannot claim the fullness of our beings as a gift of God to be grateful for.

"Let's not be afraid to look at everything that has brought us to where we are now and trust that we will soon see in it the guiding hand of a loving God."[1]

Who can know and comprehend the lessons learned and the character formed by some of life's bitter winters? Every one of us will, at one time or another, face adversity, whether it be in the form of financial reversals, illness, the loss of a loved one, consequences of our own or others' poor choices, or some other type of profound disappointment. Adversity will come to us, one and all, whether we are prepared for it or not.

Too often in tough times we yield ourselves to stress and distress, to despondency and discouragement. Certainly life is complex, the demands on our time are intense, and the temptations of the devil are sophisticated—perhaps more so today than in times past—but there is also a mindset characteristic of our day that opens us to despair. That mindset is one in which we assume, given the pleasures and luxuries of our day and age, that all should be well with us, that we should be perpetually happy. Many of us have bought into the philosophy of our pop psychology world. The truth is, life can be tough. We are not guaranteed a stress-free existence, nor did the Lord promise us a mortal life void of challenge and difficulty. There is much in the world that is glorious and beautiful and uplifting and inspiring; many of the relationships we establish, for example, are elevating and enriching—they bring the deepest of joys into our lives. But we receive our joys alongside our sorrows. Both elements of the equation come with earth life. And we knew this before we came. Such experiences "are not just to test us," Elder Paul V. Johnson pointed out. "They are vitally important to the process of putting on the divine nature. If we handle these afflictions properly, they will be consecrated for our gain." Consequently, "we must be careful that we don't resent the very things that help us put on [that] divine nature."[2]

And so we hold on, we press on, we move ahead, even though the road is not necessarily straight and the path is not necessarily clear. This is what it means to *trust the Lord*. Lessons we are to learn through our suffering may or may not be obvious. The one lesson, perhaps overarching all the rest, is patience. Elder Orson F. Whitney taught: "No pain that we suffer, no trial that we experience is wasted. It ministers to our education, to the development of such qualities as patience, faith, fortitude, and humility. All that we suffer and all that we endure, especially when we endure it patiently, builds up our characters, purifies our hearts, expands our souls, and makes us more tender and charitable, more worthy to be called the children of God."³

Facing our trials courageously and resolutely, trusting steadfastly in Christ—these things prepare us for fellowship with those who have passed the tests of mortality. Although The Church of Jesus Christ of Latter-day Saints does not subscribe to a doctrine of asceticism nor teach that we should seek after persecution or pain, persecution and pain are nonetheless the lot of the people of God in all ages. Each of us, Saint and sinner alike, becomes acquainted with the Suffering Servant through our suffering. We have been taught, by those who know best, that "all these things shall give thee experience, and shall be for thy good. The Son of Man hath descended below them all. Art thou greater than he?" (D&C 122:7–8).

No, we are not greater than he, nor should we suppose that fellowship with him who was well acquainted with grief will come through a life of ease. As the apostle Peter counseled us: "Beloved, think it not strange concerning the fiery trial which is to try you, as though some strange thing happened unto you: But rejoice, inasmuch as ye are partakers of Christ's sufferings; that, when his glory shall be revealed, ye may be glad also with exceeding joy" (1 Peter 4:12–13). As tough as it is, over time and through seasons of experience, we come to glory in our trials, for only through times of weakness and distress do we eventually emerge into a day of strength and power (2 Corinthians 12:9–10; Ether 12:27).

Each one of us either has known or will know people

who are marvelous examples, men and women of faith and determination and accomplishment, people who have changed us for the better. We learn much from their example and honor their legacy in our lives. We come to trust them, to lean upon them, to rely upon them. And yet we must always remember that mortals, no matter how impressive their credentials or how loving their manner, are still mortals, and mortals can and do occasionally let us down. "Therefore, let every man stand or fall, by himself, and not for another; or *not trusting another*" (JST, Mark 9:44; italics added).

President David O. McKay often quoted the maxim that "to be trusted is a greater compliment than to be loved."[4] In that spirit, let us be valiant in keeping the commandment: "Thou shalt love the Lord thy God with all thy heart, with all thy might, mind, and strength; and in the name of Jesus Christ thou shalt serve him" (D&C 59:5). Let us make God and his kingdom the greatest priorities in our eternal journey. With us it ought to be "the kingdom of God or nothing!" Let us praise the name and goodness of God forevermore. And let us pay our Heavenly Father and his Beloved Son an even greater compliment—let us trust them.

Chapter 14
"I NEVER KNEW YOU"

Jesus warned his followers, "Not every one that saith unto me, Lord, Lord, shall enter into the kingdom of heaven; but he that doeth the will of my Father which is in heaven" (Matthew 7:21). Christianity is about more than quaint conversation. Talk is cheap. Discipleship entails much more than saying the good word, even saying the good word to the Master.

Luke's version of the Savior's words is similarly chilling: "And why call ye me, Lord, Lord, and do not the things which I say? Whosoever cometh to me, and heareth my sayings, and doeth them, I will shew you to whom he is like: He is like a man which built an house, and digged deep, and laid the foundation on a rock: and when the flood arose, the stream beat vehemently upon that house, and could not shake it: for it was founded upon a rock. But he that heareth, and doeth not, is like a man that without a foundation built an house upon the earth; against which the stream did beat vehemently, and immediately it fell; and the ruin of that house was great" (Luke 6:46–49).

"When the kingdom of heaven comes in all its fullness," New Testament scholar Leon Morris observed, "it will not be people's profession [of belief] that counts, but their profession as shown in the way they live. . . . Jesus is not saying that it is a bad thing to say to him 'Lord, Lord,' but that it is insufficient. He has just made emphatically the point that a person's deeds show what the person is [that men are known by their fruits (Luke 6:43–46)], and he is now saying that words are not the significant thing. It is easy for anyone to profess loyalty, but to practice it is quite another thing."[1]

Paul instructed the Galatian Saints: "If we live in the Spirit, let us also walk in the Spirit" (Galatians 5:25). In today's parlance, the apostle is essentially saying: "If we talk the talk, we really ought to walk the walk." To the Romans he explained that "not the hearers of the law are just before God, but the doers of the law shall be justified" (Romans 2:13). James likewise counseled the household of faith to "be ye doers of the word, and not hearers only, deceiving your own selves" (James 1:22). John the Beloved wrote near the end of the meridian dispensation, "My little children, let us not love in word, neither in tongue; but in deed and in truth" (1 John 3:18).

Once imposing challenge we face in this enlightened age is to get the gospel from our minds to our hearts, to seek for and allow the power of the blood of Christ to transform us into men and women who *do* what they say and, more important, who *are* what they say. People who speak or teach publicly of noble values and eternal verities, who can discourse for hours upon godly attributes, and who can cite verses of scripture and quote lengthy passages or set forth steps and formulas for celestial success, but who at the same time are in any degree mischievous with another's reputation, who exercise their office in littleness or mean-spiritedness, who sow discord among their fellows (Proverbs 6:19), and who have chosen in their heart of hearts to be unrighteous in the dark—these are double-minded and unstable in all their ways (James 1:8). The gospel of Jesus Christ has yet to begin the arduous journey from their heads to their hearts. Now, to be sure, each of us lives well beneath our spiritual privileges; every one of us finds that there is some gap between our ideals and our actions. We are not speaking of striving but falling short; rather, we are addressing the far more serious concern of hypocrisy, of being purveyors but not practitioners of the word.

Many spend their lives seeking to "prove" that the resurrection of Jesus took place or to prove that the Book of Mormon story took place in this or that corner of the world, all in an effort to confirm hope through rational explanations. In the words of scientist and theologian Alister McGrath, "while we can never hope to prove conclusively that the gospel is true, we can nevertheless trust totally in the reliability of God. So many people long for certainty and find themselves totally perplexed when they cannot prove the truth of the gospel to their friends, or even to themselves.

Yet the gospel is not primarily about a set of ideas whose truth can be proved before the court of reason. *The gospel is relational. It concerns a personal transforming encounter with the living God.*"[2]

We are able to move beyond an intellectual conviction by adopting a believing attitude that impels us to action. "If any man will *do* [the Father's] will," Jesus said, "he shall *know* of the doctrine, whether it be of God, or whether I speak of myself" (John 7:17; italics added). In the same vein, Moroni pointed out that we "receive no witness until after the trial of [our] faith" (Ether 12:6), meaning, in this case, the obedience test of our beliefs. Paying a full tithing leads us to know that the promise of Malachi 3:10 is sure, not because unexpected checks come in the mail or financial security is immediately forthcoming, but perhaps more important, because we have trustingly been willing to "walk to the edge of the light, and perhaps a few steps into the darkness," discovering then that "the light will appear and move ahead of you."[3] Home and visiting teachers come to sense the profound value of Christlike service through loving and caring for those assigned to them. Men and women, boys and girls, come to know in an especially meaningful way that regularly searching the scriptures, as directed by Church leaders, brings peace and perspective and promptings and personal power. We do, and we come to know.

Faith is the total trust, complete confidence in, and ready reliance upon the perfect merits, tender mercy, and endless grace of Jesus Christ for salvation. It is a gift of the Spirit

(1 Corinthians 12:9; Moroni 10:11), a divine endowment that affirms to the human heart the identity and redemptive mission of the Savior. It is only through exercising faith in the name of Jesus Christ—meaning his power or authority, his atoning mission and work—that salvation comes to the children of men (Acts 4:12; Mosiah 3:17). The atonement of Christ "bringeth about means unto men that they may have faith unto repentance" (Alma 34:15).

Elder Orson Pratt wrote that "the grace and faith by which man is saved, are the gifts of God, having been purchased by him not by his own works, but by the blood of Christ. Had not these gifts been purchased for man, all exertions on his part would have been entirely unavailing and fruitless. Whatever course man might have pursued, he could not have atoned for one sin; it required the sacrifice of a sinless and pure Being in order to purchase the gifts of faith, repentance, and salvation for fallen man. Grace, Faith, Repentance, and Salvation, when considered in their origin, are not of man, neither by his works; man did not devise, originate, nor adopt them; superior Beings in Celestial abodes, provided these gifts, and revealed the conditions to man by which he might become a partaker of them. Therefore all boasting on the part of man is excluded. He is saved by a plan which his works did not originate—a plan of heaven, and not of earth."[4]

We as mortals simply do not have the power to fix everything that is broken. Complete restitution, as we know it, may not be possible. President Boyd K. Packer explained that "sometimes you *cannot* give back what you have taken because you don't have it to give. If you have caused others to suffer unbearably—defiled someone's virtue, for example—it is not within your power to give it back. . . .

"If you cannot undo what you have done, you are trapped. It is easy to understand how helpless and hopeless you then feel and why you might want to give up. . . . Restoring what you cannot restore, healing the wound you cannot heal, fixing that which you broke and you cannot fix is the very purpose of the atonement of Christ.

"When your desire is firm and you are willing to pay 'the uttermost farthing' (Matthew 5:25–26), the law of restitution is suspended. Your obligation is transferred to the Lord. He will settle your accounts."[5]

This strength, this enlivening influence, this spiritual change does not come to us just because we work harder or longer hours. It comes as a result of working smarter, working in conjunction with the Lord God Omnipotent. President Brigham Young testified, "My faith is, when we have done all we can, then the Lord is under obligation, and will not disappoint the faithful; He will perform the rest."[6]

Latter-day Saints have often been critical of those who emphasize salvation by grace alone, while we have often been criticized for a type of works-righteousness. The gospel is in fact a gospel covenant—a two-way promise. The Lord agrees to do for us what we could never do for ourselves—to forgive our sins, to lift our burdens, to renew our souls and re-create our nature, to raise us from the dead, and to qualify us for glory hereafter. At the same time, we promise to do what we *can* do: come unto Christ by covenant, commit our lives to him as Lord and Master, receive the appropriate ordinances (sacraments), love and serve one another, and do all in our power to put off the natural man and deny ourselves of ungodliness. We know, without question, that the power to save us, to change us, to renew our souls, is in Christ. True faith, however, always manifests itself in *faithfulness*. "When faith springs up in the heart," Brigham Young taught, "good works will follow, and good works will increase that pure faith within them."[7]

Latter-day Saints believe, with their Christian brothers and sisters, that salvation is a gift (D&C 6:13; 14:7), but we also emphasize that a gift must be received (D&C 88:33). Our receipt of the ordinances of salvation combined with our efforts to keep the commandments are extensions and manifestations of true faith. So on the one hand, Latter-day Saint scripture and prophetic teachings establish the essential truth that salvation is free (2 Nephi 2:4; 26:25, 27–28), meaning that it comes by grace, through God's unmerited favor. On the other hand, ancient and modern prophets set forth the equally vital point that works are a necessary, though insufficient, condition for salvation. We will be judged according to our works, *not according to the merits of our works* but to the extent that our works manifest to God who and what we have *become* through the transcendent powers of Christ. We are saved by grace alone, but grace is never alone.

Note the following statements from early Christian fathers (references are to volumes of *The Ante-Nicene Fathers*):

"The way of light, then, is as follows. If anyone desires to travel to the appointed place, he must be zealous in his works" (Barnabas, 1:148).

"We are justified by our works and not our words" (Clement of Rome, 1:13).

"The tree is made manifest by its fruit. So those who profess themselves to be Christians will be recognized by their conduct" (Ignatius, 1:55).

"This, then, is our reward if we will confess Him by whom we have been saved. But in what way will we confess Him? We confess Him by doing what He says, not transgressing His commandments. . . . For that reason, brethren, let us confess Him by our works, by loving one another" (Second Clement, 7:518).

"If men by their works show themselves worthy of His design, they are deemed worthy of reigning in company with Him, being delivered from corruption and suffering. This is what we have received" (Justin Martyr, 1:165).

"Let those who are not found living as He taught, be understood not to be Christians, even though they profess with the lips the teachings of Christ. For it is not those who make profession, but those who do the works, who will be saved" (Justin Martyr, 1:168).

"The matters of our religion lie in works, not in words" (Justin Martyr, 1:288).

"Whoever . . . distinguishes himself in good works will

gain the prize of everlasting life. . . . Others, attaching slight importance to the works that tend to salvation, do not make the necessary preparation for attaining to the objects of their hope" (Clement of Alexandria, 2:591).

In reality, the work of salvation of the human soul is a product of divine grace, coupled with true faith and its attendant actions. This is a synergistic relationship.[8] Thus the grace of God, provided through the intercession of the Savior, is free and yet expensive; it is *costly* grace.[9]

After we read that only those who do the will of the Father will enter the kingdom of God, we learn something of the context from the Joseph Smith Translation: "For the day soon cometh, that men shall come before me to judgment, to be judged according to their works" (JST, Matthew 7:21).

Continuing from the King James Version, we read: "Many will say to me in that day [the Day of Judgment], Lord, Lord, have we not prophesied in thy name? and in thy name have cast out devils? and in thy name done many wonderful works? And then will I profess unto them, I never knew you: depart from me, ye that work iniquity" (Matthew 7:22–23).

It is almost as though our Lord is addressing two sides of the same coin. On one side, only those who do the works of the Father have any hope of salvation in his kingdom. On the other side, clearly the performance of works alone will not open the gates of heaven. Why? Because even though certain persons—*many* persons, in the language of Christ— prophesy, exorcise demons, and otherwise perform "many wonderful works," the Lord and Redeemer, in his capacity as the keeper of the gate (2 Nephi 9:41)—the one to whom all judgment has been committed (John 3:35; 5:22)—*does not know them.*

Is this a matter of visual or cognitive recognition? Hardly. Has Jesus simply forgotten their identity? Surely not. He remembers only too well. In fact, what he remembers is what many wish he would forget. Noteworthy is that the Joseph Smith Translation of this passage alters the King James Version to clarify: "And then will I say, *Ye never knew me;* depart from me ye that work iniquity" (JST, Matthew 7:33; italics added).

The Gospel of Matthew contains what are called the three parables of preparation (Matthew 25), with the Savior speaking of a day "before the Son of Man comes" (JST, Matthew 25:1). Here the Master delivers first the parable of the ten virgins (vv. 1–13). When the unwise virgins eventually make their way to the marriage chamber, the doors have been shut: "Afterward came also the other virgins, saying, Lord, Lord, open to us. But he answered and said, Verily I say unto you, I know you not" (Matthew 25:11–12). And once again the Joseph Smith Translation alters the passage to read, "Verily I say unto you, *You know me not*" (JST Matthew 25:11; italics added). If we do not confess him, then he will not confess us to the Father in a coming day (Matthew 10:32; Luke 12:8). If in that day we have not come to know him, he will not know us.

A little more than a century before Jesus Christ came to earth, the great Nephite prophet Alma found himself, as the newly called high priest over the Church, deeply troubled as he encountered spreading transgression within the Church, "for he feared that he should do wrong in the sight of God. And it came to pass after he had poured out his whole soul to God, the voice of the Lord came to him" (Mosiah 26:13–14). What followed was marvelous counsel that we still draw upon within the restored Church.

Jehovah answered him, declaring: "This is my church; whosoever is baptized shall be baptized unto repentance. And whomsoever ye receive shall believe in my name; and him will I freely forgive.

"For it is I that taketh upon me the sins of the world; for it is I that hath created them; and it is I that granteth unto him that believeth unto the end a place at my right hand.

"For behold, in my name are they called; and *if they know me they shall come forth*, and shall have a place eternally at my right hand.

"And it shall come to pass that when the second trump shall sound *then shall they that never knew me come forth* and shall stand before me.

"And then shall they know that I am the Lord their God, that I am their Redeemer; but they would not be redeemed. And *then I will confess unto them that I never knew them*; and they shall depart into everlasting fire prepared for the devil and his angels.

"Therefore I say unto you, that he that will not hear my voice, the same shall ye not receive into my church, for him

I will not receive at the last day" (Mosiah 26:22–28; italics added).

"'I never knew you, and you never knew me!'" Elder Bruce R. McConkie paraphrased. "'Your discipleship was limited. . . . Your heart was not so centered in me as to cause you to endure to the end; and so for a time and a season you were faithful; you even worked miracles in my name; but in the end it shall be as though I never knew you.'"[10]

Why would Jesus refer to those who had paraded their many impressive works as "workers of iniquity"? (Matthew 7:23). To the extent that such deeds of wonder were accomplished for the wrong reasons—to create a following or to acquire personal gain or fame—then surely they are evil, no matter how pleasing they may appear to the eye or the ear. The New King James Version renders Matthew 7:23 this way: "Depart from Me, you who practice lawlessness" (compare also the English Standard Version). Other modern translations render this passage as "Away from me, you evildoers" (New International Version, Today's New International Version, New Revised Standard Version, New American Bible, New Jerusalem Bible) or "Out of my sight; your deeds are evil!" (Revised English Bible).

Our deeds that are apart from God, any efforts separated from Christ, noble labors performed independent of Deity and his Spirit are essentially evil (Moroni 7:8–11). Isaiah wrote, "But we are all as an unclean thing, and all our righteousnesses are as filthy rags" (Isaiah 64:6). Truly, a church that carries the name of Christ and is built upon the gospel of Jesus Christ will show forth the Father's works in it. On the other hand, the works of men or the works of the devil are ephemeral and fleeting. The risen Lord declared to his American Hebrews that "they have joy in their works for a season, and by and by the end cometh, and they are hewn down and cast into the fire, from whence there is no return" (3 Nephi 27:10–11).

Perhaps my favorite rendition of this passage from Matthew is provided in Evangelical pastor and writer Eugene H. Peterson's helpful paraphrase, *The Message:* "Knowing the correct password—saying 'Master, Master,' for instance—isn't going to get you anywhere with me. What is required is serious obedience—*doing* what my Father wills. I can see it now—at the Final Judgment thousands strutting up to me and saying 'Master, we preached the Message, we bashed the demons, our God-sponsored projects had everyone talking.' And do you know what I am going to say? 'You missed the boat. All you did was use me to make yourselves important. You don't impress me one bit. You're out of here.'"[11]

We are not called upon to perform the works of righteousness to pay back what we owe to Jesus Christ. We do not receive the ordinances of salvation, attend to our responsibilities within the Church, or serve one another through charitable actions in order to supplement the finished work of Christ. In reality, a Christ supplemented is a Christ supplanted. Salvation, or eternal life, is free; it is the greatest of all the gifts of God (2 Nephi 2:4; D&C 6:13; 14:7). "What doth it profit a man if a gift is bestowed upon him, and he receive not the gift? Behold, he rejoices not in that which is given unto him, neither rejoices in him who is the giver of the gift" (D&C 88:33).

As we noted earlier, Elder Dallin H. Oaks explained that "the Final Judgment is not just an evaluation of a sum total of good and evil acts—what we have *done*. It is an acknowledgment of the final effect of our acts and thoughts—what we have *become*. It is not enough for anyone just to go through the motions. The commandments, ordinances, and covenants of the gospel are not a list of deposits required to be made in some heavenly account. The gospel of Jesus Christ is a plan that shows us how to become what our Heavenly father desires us to become. . . .

"We are challenged to move through a process of conversion," Elder Oaks continues, "toward that status and condition called eternal life. This is achieved not just by doing what is right, but by doing it for the right reason—for the pure love of Christ. . . . The reason charity never fails and the reason charity is greater than even the most significant acts of goodness . . . is that charity, 'the pure love of Christ' (Moroni 7:47), is not an *act* but a *condition* or state of being. Charity is attained through a succession of acts that result in a conversion. Charity is something one becomes."[12]

In other words, part of that conversion of which Elder Oaks spoke is a change in attitude, a change in motive, a change in desire—all undergirded by a change in heart. Each of us performs good works for a variety of reasons; our place on the continuum of motivation for service may be anywhere

from earthly reward to good companionship to fear of pun-
ishment to loyalty and duty to a hope of eternal reward to
charity.[13] As we seek for and cultivate the Spirit of God in
our lives, that sacred influence gradually educates our desires, strengthens our consciences, buttresses our judgment,
enhances our wisdom, refines our character, strengthens
our hope in Christ, and transforms why we do what we do.
Through this divine metamorphosis, we gain the mind of
Christ (1 Corinthians 2:16).

We begin to attend church because we yearn to partake
of the holy sacrament and commune with Deity. We search
the scriptures not only because the prophets have counseled
us to do so but because we experience something akin to
worship during our private devotions. We avoid worldly and
degrading movies, TV programs, music, and computer use
not just because we might get into trouble but, more important, because God is a Man of Holiness (Moses 6:57) and
we desire to be holy (Leviticus 11:44; 1 Peter 1:16). In short,
the truly converted soul loves our Heavenly Father, loves
Jesus the Christ, and keeps the commandments as an expression of that love and of an undying gratitude for the great
plan of happiness. "For this is the love of God," John writes,
"that we keep his commandments: and his commandments
are not grievous" (1 John 5:3), meaning they are neither op-
pressive nor burdensome. "Christ longs to nourish our minds
with his truth," Dr. Alister McGrath has written, "to raise
our imaginations to new heights through his beauty; to open
our hearts to his love; to surrender our wills to his purpose;

and to allow his holiness to challenge the way we behave. In every way, Christ lays the most fundamental challenge to the root of our lives: in all things, he asks us to submit our entire being to his wise and loving rule. To know Christ is to begin this process of change and renewal."[14]

At the beginning of his great High Priestly Prayer, his intercession for all his disciples, then and now, a prayer that brought the Last Supper to a close, Jesus spoke: "And this is life eternal, that they might know thee the only true God, and Jesus Christ, whom thou hast sent" (John 17:3). Life eternal comes to those who know their God, not just those who know *about* their God. Everlasting life comes to those who come to know him because they have served him faithfully (Mosiah 5:15). Salvation comes to those who have yielded their hearts unto the Almighty and through that means have been sanctified (Helaman 3:35). Knowing God towers above all earthly attainments. Knowing Christ brings sublime joy and a settled fearlessness that empowers us to engage and endure any trial or trauma or tragedy. Indeed, as the apostle Paul declared, "I count all things but loss for the excellency of the knowledge of Christ Jesus my Lord" (Philippians 3:8). The knowledge of our God—experiential knowledge, covenant knowledge, relational knowledge—transcends all other discovery, all other intellectual acquisition. It is the knowledge that saves.

To know Christ is to have total trust in him, to have a complete confidence in him, to exercise a ready reliance upon him. Knowing Christ enables us to face life's vicissitudes optimistically, knowing also that our divine Redeemer has "prepared a house for man, yea, even among the mansions of [our] Father, in which man might have a more excellent hope" (Ether 12:32). We are strangers here, and with the infusion of Christian character comes a divine homesickness that whispers we will never be at rest until we rest with our Lord.

President Thomas S. Monson has encouraged us: "Let us, in the performance of our duty, follow in the footsteps of the Master. As you and I walk the pathway Jesus walked, let us listen for the sound of sandaled feet. Let us reach out for the Carpenter's hand. Then we shall come to know Him. . . . He commands, and to those who obey Him, whether they be wise or simple, He will reveal Himself in the toils, the conflicts, the sufferings that they shall pass through in His fellowship; and they shall learn by their own experience who He is.

"We will discover He is more than the Babe in Bethlehem, more than the carpenter's son, more than the greatest teacher ever to live. We will come to know Him as the Son of God, our Savior and our Redeemer."[15]

Those who nurture a lifelong trust and confidence in Jesus Christ and sustain their effort to keep the commandments and walk in the Light will come to know their Lord and become partakers of the heavenly gift. The call of the lowly Nazarene is in fact a call to a higher righteousness, an invitation to defy shallow categories and transcend false dichotomies: it is a call for boldness coupled with tenderness, for obedience coupled with reliance, for dynamic individualism coupled with unconditional surrender; it is a call to be the light of the world and the salt of the earth, coupled with genuine humility. In short, we come to know the Master as our lives more closely parallel his life, as we gain "the mind of Christ" (1 Corinthians 2:16).

Chapter 15

RETROSPECT AND PROSPECT

President David O. McKay taught, "No man can sincerely resolve to apply to his daily life the teachings of Jesus of Nazareth without sensing a change in his own nature."[1] To choose Christ is to choose to be changed. Indeed, the glorious message of the gospel of Jesus Christ is that we can be better than we are, that we can change. The quest to become more like our Lord and Savior—to be more spiritually attentive, more personally sensitive, more tender and gracious— ought to be the righteous focus of every Latter-day Saint. What, then, can I do?

1. *Self-denial.* If I find myself drawn to addictive patterns, then I can choose to avoid questionable locations, potentially compromising situations, and perhaps even people who prove more a temptation than a strength. If it becomes clear that my repeated insistence on being right is becoming an obstacle to my relationship with friends and family, then maybe

I can learn to remain quiet, keep my comments to myself, allow the conversation to go forward without my contribution. Or, if I notice that time after time my speech and behavior at athletic contests are less than Christian, it just may be necessary to absent myself occasionally.

During his mortal ministry, Jesus called upon those who follow him to deny themselves, to use personal restraint and moral discipline, to take up their cross daily (Luke 9:23). "And now for a man to take up his cross," the Master clarified, "is to deny himself all ungodliness, and every worldly lust, and keep my commandments" (JST, Matthew 16:24; see also 3 Nephi 12:29–30).

Discipleship is always a result of spiritual conditioning. We can never enjoy the blessings of self-mastery if we are slaves to our passions and appetites. As President McKay explained, "Spirituality is the consciousness of victory over self, and of communion with the Infinite."[2] There is something infinitely sublime about the quiet confidence, the peaceful assurance of God's pleasure, that comes into our hearts and minds through enjoying victory over the flesh.

2. Emulation. By searching the holy scriptures, we discover God's constitution for goodness and a happy life. The principles, precepts, and parameters found therein can provide a lifelong course of instruction on such matters as how to become and remain a covenant person, how to keep God first in our lives, how to avoid the perils of the prosperity cycle, how to attend to the needs of the less fortunate and ease their burdens, how to repent of our sins and enjoy the cleansing power of the blood of Christ, how to live a sane and balanced life, how to prepare for what lies ahead. The scriptures also teach us what God is like: how he extends to each of us his ongoing and everlasting tender mercies, what he commends and what he condemns, his infinite patience and longsuffering with finite and struggling mortals, and his special watchcare over the outcast and the excluded. If I decide that I want to be a more godly person, it only makes sense that I should search the scriptures, the revelations, to discover the attributes and qualities of our Lord that seem so very desirable.

We can ask, "What would Jesus do?" whenever we find ourselves in circumstances that require an answer or an action. And in many cases we will discover in the Testaments (the Bible and Book of Mormon) specific deeds or determinations of Jehovah or Jesus Christ that point the way. Further, we can meditate on the principles being taught, principles that can be applied to a myriad of situations. Such a course in life will gradually help us comprehend why the imitation of Christ, the emulation of him who never took a backward step, who did all things wisely and well, is one of the highest forms of worship. "'What would Jesus do?' or 'What would he have me do?' are the paramount personal questions of this life," President Ezra Taft Benson observed. "Walking in His way is the greatest achievement of life. That man or woman is most truly successful whose life most closely parallels that of the Master."[3]

3. *Transformation*. No doubt we can pursue the path of

Christ-likeness through persistence. But it becomes painfully apparent after a while that sheer grit and willpower can do only so much, that dogged determination has its limits, and that doubling and tripling our efforts may well prove in the long run to be both physically exhausting and spiritually counterproductive. Our Lord and Redeemer has called upon us to come unto him, to be yoked to him, and to experience the refreshing respite that derives from surrender to him (Matthew 11:28–30). He has, through Simon Peter, invited each of us to "[cast] all your care upon him; for he careth for you" (1 Peter 5:7). Of course he cares for us; he loves us, perfectly. More poignantly, however, is the sweet promise that if we lay our burdens at his feet, he will care *for us;* that is, if we can learn to trust him, rely upon him, and have complete confidence in him (we call this state of being *faith*), he will do the worrying, the fretting, and the caring—for us. In the words of the great defender of the Christian faith, C. S. Lewis, we keep trying but we are "trying in a new way, a less worried way."[4]

As we strive to cultivate the gift of the Holy Ghost, to enjoy the cleansing and empowering presence of the third member of the Godhead, not only will our hearts be renewed but our desires will be educated, our energies extended, and our capacity expanded. The apostle Paul cautioned the early Saints not to be "conformed to this world: but be ye transformed by the renewing of your mind" (Romans 12:2). This comes about through that *grace* of which holy writ attests, the sustaining influence and enabling power of the Almighty that equips us to do what we could never do on our own. It is a gift of God, a gift that must be sought for, pleaded for, and accepted.

Paul taught that the "works of the flesh," the works of the natural man, the by-products of an unredeemed and unchanged heart, are deeds that lead to decay and destruction. On the other hand, the "fruit of the Spirit" is those divine qualities, those Christlike attributes that in course of time automatically flow from a transformed heart and a life centered in Christ—love, joy, peace, longsuffering, gentleness, goodness, faith, meekness, and temperance, or self-control (Galatians 5:19–24).

In summary, we strive to deny ourselves of ungodliness. We yearn to have our walk and talk be like unto those of our Exemplar, the prototype of all saved beings.[5] And we seek for and obtain a nature, a disposition, that no longer finds worldliness attractive, that no longer takes its cues from a fickle society, that no longer feels comfortable in Babylon. And thus when Jesus Christ returns in glory he will be welcomed by those called the children of God, those who see him as he is, for they will be like him (1 John 3:1–2; Moroni 7:48).

I am a Christian, a follower of the lowly Nazarene who will yet return to planet Earth to reign as King of kings and Lord of lords. I believe with all my heart in the divine Sonship of Jesus. He is the Lord of my life, my Savior and my Redeemer. On scores of occasions individuals have questioned my Christianity. As President Boyd K. Packer noted: "There has been no end to opposition. There are misinterpretations and misrepresentations of us and of our history, some of it mean-spirited and certainly contrary to the teachings of Jesus Christ and His gospel. Sometimes clergy, even ministerial organizations, oppose us. They do what we would never do. We do not attack or criticize or oppose others as they do us.

"Even today there are those preposterous stories handed down and repeated so many times they are believed. . . . Strangest of all, otherwise intelligent people claim we are not Christian. This shows that they know little or nothing about us. It is a true principle that you cannot lift yourself by putting others down."[6]

I believe in the historical Jesus. I accept as accurate and true the accounts of his ministry in the four Gospels of the New Testament. I believe in the miracle surrounding the birth of the Christ, that he was born of the Virgin Mary. I believe that Jesus of Nazareth lived during the time of Tiberius Caesar, ministered and taught in the days of the high priests Annas and Caiaphas, and died at the hands of Jewish leaders and Roman soldiers under Pontius Pilate.

Jesus Christ grew to maturity, began his ministry, taught his gospel, called people to repentance, announced his kingdom, chose and ordained apostles, organized his church, and declared plainly who he was. He performed miracles—such as demonstrating power over the elements, causing the blind to see and the deaf to hear, and even raising the dead. Jesus was the Master Teacher, but he was more than a teacher. He loved those among whom he walked and ministered—saint and sinner alike—but he was more than a kindly and gentle soul. He was the Christ, the Promised Messiah, the One sent to "preach good tidings unto the meek; . . . to bind up the brokenhearted, to proclaim liberty to the captives, and the opening of the prison to them that are bound" (Isaiah 61:1; compare Luke 4:18–19). Jesus was fully human and fully God (John 10:17–18; compare 2 Nephi 2:8). He was the Son of God, but he was also God the Son. And if it were not so, he could not save us.

I believe the fall of Adam and Eve to be part of God's sovereign plan, and I readily acknowledge that the Fall was real and universal, that it affected humankind and all other forms of life on earth. All things are born, and all things must die. Further, because of the Fall we often choose to yield to sin, to live in a manner contrary to the will of the Almighty. No one—not the greatest prophet or the mightiest apostle—has lived a sin-free life, save only Jesus Christ. All have sinned. All fall short of the glory of God (Romans 3:23). All are in need of pardoning mercy. Neither death nor sin can be overcome by anything men or women can devise. Deliverance can come only through the love and forgiveness of One possessed of the power of God, One who traversed life's paths without committing sin (Hebrews 4:15; 1 Peter 2:22). The reconciliation of fallen, finite persons to a holy and infinite God is accomplished through the mediation of Jesus Christ, through the implementation of a plan of salvation, through an infinite atonement. If there had been no atonement or plan of redemption, no amount of good on man's part could make up for their absence. Jesus Christ is our only hope.

I believe that in the act of atonement Christ offered himself as a ransom for the sins of all humankind (Matthew 20:28; 1 Timothy 2:6), that he suffered and bled and died on our behalf and thereby satisfied the demands of divine justice. As a Latter-day Saint, I believe his redemptive suffering began in the Garden of Gethsemane, where he experienced something he had never known before—an alienation from his Father, a withdrawal of his Father's sustaining Spirit. Upon his shoulders fell the burden and weight of the sins and pains of all humankind. As the apostle Paul taught, Christ "became sin" for us, in order that we might receive the righteousness of God through him (2 Corinthians 5:21). "Christ hath redeemed us from the curse of the law," Paul wrote on another occasion, "being made a curse for us" (Galatians 3:13). Jehovah thereby could speak prophetically through Isaiah, "I have trodden the winepress alone . . . and their blood shall be sprinkled upon my garments" (Isaiah 63:3). Or, as He stated in the Doctrine and Covenants, "I have overcome and have trodden the wine-press alone, even the wine-press of the fierceness of the wrath of Almighty God" (D&C 76:107; see also 88:106; 133:50).

The atoning suffering was not fully accomplished in Gethsemane, however; rather, what began in the garden was completed on the cross of Calvary. On what we traditionally call that first Good Friday, between the hours of noon and 3:00 P.M., all the agonies of the night before recurred.

The Father's Spirit was withdrawn, causing the Sinless One to cry out in agony, "My God, my God, why hast thou forsaken me?" (Matthew 27:46). We thus speak of our Lord's atoning sacrifice, his ultimate passion, as taking place both in Gethsemane and on Golgotha.

Jesus' body was taken down from the cross and placed in the tomb of Joseph of Arimathea. On the third day, on that first Easter morning, in a manner miraculous and thus incomprehensible to us all, Jesus rose from the dead. His spirit and body were reunited to form a resurrected, immortal, and glorified being. Jesus thereby became the "firstfruits of them that slept" (1 Corinthians 15:20). And because Jesus rose from the dead, we have a supernal hope in the immortality of the soul, the knowledge that death is not the end, the assurance that we will live again: "For since by man [Adam] came death, by man [Jesus] came also the resurrection of the dead. For as in Adam all die, even so in Christ shall all be made alive" (1 Corinthians 15:21–22).

Salvation, or eternal life, is described in the Doctrine and Covenants as the greatest of all the gifts of God (D&C 6:13; 14:7). The Book of Mormon teaches that "salvation is free" (2 Nephi 2:4). The gospel of Jesus Christ represents a covenant. God agrees to do for us those things we could never do for ourselves—forgive our sins, cleanse and renew our minds and hearts, and raise us from the dead in the resurrection in a glorified, immortal condition. These are the acts of God, acts of grace. The Book of Mormon clearly teaches that "since man had fallen he could not merit anything of himself" (Alma 22:14) and "there is no flesh that can dwell in the presence of God, save it be through the merits, and mercy, and grace of the Holy Messiah" (2 Nephi 2:8). Grace is unmerited divine favor, unearned divine assistance, enabling power, heavenly help to accomplish tasks that we could never accomplish when left to our own meager resources. We will be forever grateful for the grace of God; indeed, we have been instructed to rely wholly, to rely alone upon the merits of him who is mighty to save (2 Nephi 31:19; Moroni 6:4).

The other side of the covenant is what we as mortals agree to do. We gladly acknowledge the gifts of God, but gifts must be received to be enjoyed. We receive the blessings of the Atonement by exercising faith in the Lord Jesus Christ: we come to believe what he says and rely upon what he has done, is now doing, and will yet do for us. We trust him, yield our hearts to him, and surrender our will to him. Repentance and baptism and the ordinances of salvation naturally flow from faith, as does a dedicated life, a discipleship that demonstrates faithfulness (Luke 9:23; John 14:15; James 2:17–20). By living faithfully and keeping the commandments of God, we can receive a fuller measure of blessings here and hereafter, but even these greater blessings are freely given of him and are not technically earned by us. In short, good works, while a vital part of our discipleship, are not sufficient to save us.

I know that men and women cannot, simply cannot, save themselves. At the same time, I believe that good works are important, that they evidence what kind of people we really are, that how we live is a visible witness to what we believe.

Conversion to Christ cannot be separated from Christian discipleship. The Master himself called upon people in his day (and ours) to repent and change their ways. "If any man will come after me," he said, "let him deny himself, and take up his cross daily, and follow me" (Luke 9:23).

The Savior extended the ultimate challenge to his followers when he beckoned, "Be ye therefore perfect, even as your Father which is in heaven is perfect" (Matthew 5:48). To be perfect is to be made whole, complete, mature, finished, fully formed. Such a state comes only through the Atonement, for we are "made perfect" (D&C 76:69)—perfected—in Christ (Moroni 10:32). Through the precious blood of our Lord, we become "new creature[s]" (2 Corinthians 5:17; Mosiah 27:26); "joint-heirs with Christ" (Romans 8:17); and "partakers of the divine nature" (2 Peter 1:4). While we are unable now to fathom what life in the presence of God will be like, "we know that, when he shall appear, we shall be like him; for we shall see him as he is" (1 John 3:1–2; Moroni 7:48).

"In recent years," Elder Bruce C. Hafen stated, "we Latter-day Saints have been teaching, singing, and testifying much more about the Savior Jesus Christ. I rejoice that we are rejoicing more. As we 'talk [more] of Christ' (2 Nephi 25:26), the gospel's doctrinal fulness will come out of obscurity." Elder Hafen spoke boldly of the spread of falsehood relative to Latter-day Saint doctrine. He drew our attention to the fact that "the adversary is engaged in one of history's greatest cover-ups, trying to persuade people that this Church knows least—when in fact it knows most—about how our relationship with Christ makes true Christians of us."[7]

I rejoice in the gospel, "the glad tidings . . . that he came into the world, even Jesus, to be crucified for the world, and to bear the sins of the world, and to sanctify the world, and to cleanse it from all unrighteousness" (D&C 76:40–41). In him I have total trust. In him I have complete confidence. Upon him I rely everlastingly. I worship him, as I do the Father, in the full majesty of his Godhood. This good news Latter-day Saints share with professing Christians throughout the world. My heart resonates with the words of Paul: "Thanks be to God, [who] giveth us the victory through our Lord Jesus Christ" (1 Corinthians 15:57). In one sense, the battle with Satan and sin is already won, for Christ has crushed the serpent's head. We may not know what the final score will be, but we know who will be the Victor. And those individuals who have cast their lot with the Master, have given their hearts and consecrated their wills to him, will overcome the world by faith (D&C 76:53), vanquish the devil by the blood of the Lamb and the power of their testimony (Revelation 12:11), live confidently and victoriously in this world, and dwell everlastingly and joyously with their families in the presence of the Father and the Son, worlds without end.

NOTES

Chapter 1
After the Image of Our Own God

1. *Teachings of the Prophet Joseph Smith*, 298.

2. Warren, *Purpose-Driven Life*, 34.

3. Lewis, *Letters to Malcolm*, 29–30; italics added.

4. Packer, "Light of Christ," 11.

5. *Teachings of Spencer W. Kimball*, 76–77; italics added.

6. Benson, "Great Commandment—Love the Lord," 4.

Chapter 2
People Ought to Know

1. *Teachings of the Prophet Joseph Smith*, 121.

2. Packer, "Mediator," 56; italics added.

3. Hinckley, "Speaking Today," 73.

Chapter 3
If Jesus Is the Answer, What's the Question?

1. Packer, "Spiritual Crocodiles," 32; italics added.

2. Holland, *Trusting Jesus*, 68.

3. *Hymns*, no. 129.

4. Francis Thompson, "The Hound of Heaven," in *The Oxford Book of*

Mystical Verse, edited by D. H. S. Nicholson and A. H. E. Lee (Oxford: Clarendon Press, 1917); available online at www.bartleby.com.

5. Whitney, in Conference Report, April 1929, 110; italics added.

6. *Hymns*, no. 85.

7. Larson and Larson, *Diary of Charles L. Walker*, 1:595–96; italics added.

8. *Teachings of Gordon B. Hinckley*, 152.

CHAPTER 4
"Jesus Loves Me, This I Know"

1. See Yancey, *What's So Amazing about Grace?* 67.

2. McConkie, *Mortal Messiah*, 4:123.

3. Maxwell, "Willing to Submit," 72.

4. *Teachings of the Prophet Joseph Smith*, 188.

5. Maxwell, "Willing to Submit," 72–73.

6. *Hymns*, no. 194.

7. McConkie, *Mortal Messiah*, 4:125; see also McConkie, "The Purifying Power of Gethsemane," 9.

8. Brigham Young, in *Journal of Discourses*, 3:206; italics added.

9. Talmage, *Jesus the Christ*, 613.

10. *Lectures on Faith*, 59; compare Hebrews 12:3.

11. McConkie, *Mortal Messiah*, 4:124.

12. *Teachings of Ezra Taft Benson*, 14.

CHAPTER 5
How Good Do I Have to Be?

1. Oaks, "Challenge to Become," 32.

2. Kimball, "Let Us Move Forward and Upward," 82; italics added.

3. Hinckley, "This Is the Work of the Master," 71.

4. Stanley, *Am I Good Enough?* 44.

5. See Stanley, *How Good Is Good Enough?* 63.

6. *Discourses of Wilford Woodruff*, 5.

CHAPTER 6
That's Not Fair!

1. Holland, "Other Prodigal," 63; italics added.

2. McCullough, *If Grace Is So Amazing*, 16.

3. Capon, *Parables of Judgment*, 53. Quoted in McCullough, *If Grace Is So Amazing*, 16.

4. Oaks, "Challenge to Become," 34; italics added.

5. Stanley, *Am I Good Enough?* 81–82; italics added.

Chapter 7
How We Worship

1. McConkie, *Promised Messiah*, 566–67.

2. *Teachings of Ezra Taft Benson*, 67.

3. *Teachings of Spencer W. Kimball*, 2.

4. Holland, "Only True God and Jesus Christ Whom He Hath Sent," 40.

5. Holland, "Grandeur of God," 71, 72.

6. *Teachings of Spencer W. Kimball*, 7–8.

7. *Hymns*, no. 67.

Chapter 8
"Gently Raise the Sacred Strain"

1. *Hymns*, ix.

2. *Hymns*, no. 270.

3. Stackhouse, *Evangelical Landscapes*, 16.

4. Packer, "Inspiring Music—Worthy Thoughts," 25.

5. *Hymns*, no. 131; italics added.

Chapter 9
The Imitation of Christ

1. Janice Kapp Perry, "I'm Trying to Be like Jesus," *Children's Songbook*, 78.

2. Lucado, *Just like Jesus*, 3.

3. *Hymns*, no. 240.

4. Lewis, *Mere Christianity*, 169.

5. McConkie, *Promised Messiah*, 568.

Chapter 10
Our Climb to Higher Ground

1. Lee, "Stand Ye in Holy Places," 123.

2. *Hymns*, no. 292.

3. Smith, *Sharing the Gospel*, 42.

4. John Taylor, in *Journal of Discourses*, 6:19.

5. Dew, "Our Only Chance," 66.

6. Lewis, *Weight of Glory*, 106.

7. *Teachings of the Prophet Joseph Smith*, 121.

8. Wirthlin, "Journey to Higher Ground," 18–19.

CHAPTER 11
THE OBJECT OF OUR WORSHIP

1. Lewis, *Problem of Pain*, 35–36.

2. Long, "God Is Not Nice," 49–50; Ken Woodward was for many years the religion editor at *Newsweek*.

3. Manning, *Ruthless Trust*, 107.

4. Lewis, *Mere Christianity*, 56.

5. Lewis, *Mere Christianity*, 137.

6. See page 5 of this volume; Lewis, *Letters to Malcolm*, 29–30.

7. Manning, *Importance of Being Foolish*, 174.

8. Ballard, "Building Bridges of Understanding," 66–67.

9. Manning, *Importance of Being Foolish*, 51.

10. Lewis, *Letters to Malcolm*, 13.

11. Ballard, "Building Bridges of Understanding," 65.

CHAPTER 12
STRIVING AND STEADY

1. Oaks, "Family History," 6–7.

2. Smith, *Gospel Doctrine*, 122.

3. Smith, *Gospel Doctrine*, 116–17.

4. Lee, in Conference Report, April 1970, 55; quoted in Clark, *Messages of the First Presidency*, 4:285–86.

5. McConkie, *Doctrines of the Restoration*, 232; italics added.

6. Packer, "That All May Be Edified," 338.

7. Kimball, *Faith Precedes the Miracle*, 255–56.

8. Larsen, "Looking beyond the Mark," 11.

CHAPTER 13
TRUSTING CHRIST

1. Nouwen, *Bread for the Journey*, 12.

2. Johnson, "More Than Conquerors," 78, 80.

3. Orson F. Whitney, quoted in Kimball, *Faith Precedes the Miracle*, 98.

4. McKay, *True to the Faith*, 272.

Chapter 14
"I Never Knew You"

1. Morris, *Gospel According to Matthew*, 178–79.

2. McGrath, *Knowing Christ*, 234; italics added.

3. Harold B. Lee, quoted in Packer, *Holy Temple*, 184.

4. Pratt, "The True Faith," in *Series of Pamphlets*, or in *Orson Pratt's Works*, 51.

5. Packer, "Brilliant Morning of Forgiveness," 19–20.

6. Brigham Young, in *Journal of Discourses*, 4:91.

7. Brigham Young, in *Journal of Discourses*, 3:155.

8. See Lewis, *Mere Christianity*, 131–32.

9. Bonhoeffer, *Cost of Discipleship*, 47–48.

10. McConkie, *Mortal Messiah*, 2:172–73.

11. Peterson, *Message*, 1757.

12. Oaks, "The Challenge to Become," 32, 34; see also Bednar, "Becoming a Missionary," 44–47, for an application to missionary work of the principle of "becoming."

13. See Oaks, *Pure in Heart*, 37–49.

14. McGrath, *Knowing Christ*, 17–18.

15. Monson, "Call of Duty," 39.

Chapter 15
Retrospect and Prospect

1. McKay, in Conference Report, April 1962, 7.

2. McKay, *Gospel Ideals*, 390.

3. Benson, *Come unto Christ*, 47.

4. Lewis, *Mere Christianity*, 130–31.

5. *Lectures on Faith*, 75–76.

6. Packer, "Defense and a Refuge," 87.

7. Hafen, "Atonement," 97, 98.

SOURCES

The Ante-Nicene Fathers. 10 vols. Edited by Alexander Roberts and James Donaldson. Grand Rapids, Mich.: Eerdmans, 1981.

Ballard, M. Russell. "Building Bridges of Understanding." *Ensign,* June 1998, 62–68.

Bednar, David A. "Becoming a Missionary." *Ensign,* Nov. 2005, 44–47.

Benson, Ezra Taft. *Come unto Christ.* Salt Lake City: Deseret Book, 1983.

———. "The Great Commandment—Love the Lord." *Ensign,* May 1988, 4–6.

———. *The Teachings of Ezra Taft Benson.* Salt Lake City: Bookcraft, 1988.

Bonhoeffer, Dietrich. *The Cost of Discipleship.* New York: Macmillan, 1963.

Capon, Robert. *Parables of Judgment.* Grand Rapids, Mich.: Eerdmans, 1989.

Dew, Sheri L. "Our Only Chance." *Ensign,* May 1999, 66–67.

Diary of Charles Lowell Walker. Edited by A. Karl Larson and Katherine Larson. Logan, Utah: Utah State University Press, 1980.

Hafen, Bruce C. "The Atonement: All for All." *Ensign*, May 2004, 97–99.

Hinckley, Gordon B. "Speaking Today: Excerpts from Recent Addresses of President Gordon B. Hinckley." *Ensign*, Feb. 1998, 73–78.

———. *Teachings of Gordon B. Hinckley*. Salt Lake City: Deseret Book, 1997.

———. "This Is the Work of the Master." *Ensign*, May 1995, 69–71.

Holland, Jeffrey R. "The Grandeur of God." *Ensign*, Nov. 2003, 70–73.

———. "The Only True God and Jesus Christ Whom He Hath Sent." *Ensign*, Nov. 2007, 40–42.

———. "The Other Prodigal." *Ensign*, May 2002, 62–64.

———. *Trusting Jesus*. Salt Lake City: Deseret Book, 2003.

Hymns of The Church of Jesus Christ of Latter-day Saints. Salt Lake City: The Church of Jesus Christ of Latter-day Saints, 1985.

Johnson, Paul V. "More Than Conquerors through Him that Loved Us." *Ensign*, May 2011, 78–80.

Journal of Discourses. 26 vols. London: Latter-day Saints' Book Depot, 1854–86.

Kimball, Spencer W. *Faith Precedes the Miracle*. Salt Lake City: Deseret Book, 1972.

———. "Let us Move Forward and Upward." *Ensign*, May 1979, 82–84.

———. *The Teachings of Spencer W. Kimball*. Edited by Edward L. Kimball. Salt Lake City: Bookcraft, 1982.

Larsen, Dean L. "Looking beyond the Mark." *Ensign*, Nov. 1987, 11–12.

Lectures on Faith. Salt Lake City: Deseret Book, 1985.

Lee, Harold B. In Conference Report. April 1970, 54–57, quoted in *Messages of the First Presidency of The Church of Jesus Christ of Latter-day Saints*, edited by James R. Clark, 6 vols. (Salt Lake City: Bookcraft, 1965–75), 4:285–86.

———. "Stand Ye in Holy Places." *Ensign*, July 1973, 121–24.

Lewis, C. S. *Letters to Malcolm, Chiefly on Prayer*. New York: Harcourt Brace, 1992.

———. *Mere Christianity*. New York: Simon & Schuster, 1996.

———. *The Problem of Pain.* New York: Simon & Schuster, 1996.

———. *The Weight of Glory.* New York: Simon & Schuster, 1996.

Long, D. Steven. "God Is Not Nice." In D. Brent Laytham, ed., *God Is Not . . .* Grand Rapids: Brazos Press, 2004.

Lucado, Max. *Just like Jesus.* Nashville: W Publishing Group, 2003.

Manning, Brennan. *The Importance of Being Foolish: How to Think like Jesus.* San Francisco: HarperSanFrancisco, 2005.

———. *Ruthless Trust: The Ragamuffin's Path to God.* San Francisco: HarperSanFrancisco, 2000.

Maxwell, Neal A. "Willing to Submit." *Ensign,* May 1985, 70–73.

McConkie, Bruce R. *Doctrines of the Restoration: Sermons and Writings of Bruce R. McConkie.* Edited and arranged by Mark L. McConkie. Salt Lake City: Bookcraft, 1989.

———. *The Mortal Messiah.* 4 vols. Salt Lake City: Deseret Book, 1979–81.

———. *The Promised Messiah: The First Coming of Christ.* Salt Lake City: Deseret Book, 1981.

———. "The Purifying Power of Gethsemane." *Ensign,* May 1985, 9–11.

McCullough, Donald. *If Grace Is So Amazing, Why Don't We Like It?* San Francisco: Jossey-Bass, 2005.

———. *The Trivialization of God: The Dangerous Illusion of a Manageable Deity.* Colorado Springs, Colo.: NavPress, 1995.

McGrath, Alister. *Knowing Christ.* New York: Doubleday Galilee, 2002.

McKay, David O. In Conference Report, Apr. 1962, 7.

———. *Gospel Ideals: Selections from the Discourses of David O. McKay.* Salt Lake City: Deseret News Press, 1953.

———. *True to the Faith: Sermons and Writings of David O. McKay.* Compiled by Llewelyn R. McKay. Salt Lake City: Bookcraft, 1966.

Monson, Thomas S. "The Call of Duty." *Ensign,* May 1986, 37–39.

Morris, Leon. *The Gospel according to Matthew.* Grand Rapids, Mich.: Eerdmans, 1992.

The New Shorter Oxford English Dictionary. 2 vols. Oxford: Clarendon Press, 1993.

Nouwen, Henri J. M. *Bread for the Journey*. San Francisco: HarperSanFrancisco, 1997.

Oaks, Dallin H. "The Challenge to Become." *Ensign*, Nov. 2000, 32–34.

———. "Family History: 'In Wisdom and Order.'" *Ensign*, June 1989, 6–8.

———. *Pure in Heart*. Salt Lake City: Bookcraft, 1988.

Packer, Boyd K. "The Brilliant Morning of Forgiveness." *Ensign*, Nov. 1995, 18–21.

———. "A Defense and a Refuge." *Ensign*, Nov. 2006, 85–88.

———. *The Holy Temple*. Salt Lake City: Bookcraft, 1980.

———. "Inspiring Music—Worthy Thoughts." *Ensign*, Jan. 1974, 25–28.

———. "The Light of Christ." *Ensign*, Apr. 2005, 8–14.

———. "The Mediator." *Ensign*, May 1977, 54–56.

———. "Spiritual Crocodiles." *Ensign*, May 1976, 30–32.

———. *"That All May Be Edified": Talks, Sermons & Commentary by Boyd K. Packer*. Salt Lake City: Bookcraft, 1982.

Perry, Janice Kapp. "I'm Trying to Be like Jesus." *Children's Songbook of The Church of Jesus Christ of Latter-day Saints*. Salt Lake City: The Church of Jesus Christ of Latter-day Saints, 1989.

Peterson, Eugene H. *The Message: The Bible in Contemporary Language*. Colorado Springs, Colo.: NavPress, 2002.

Pratt, Orson. *A Series of Pamphlets*. Liverpool: F. D. Richards, 1852.

———. *Orson Pratt's Works on the Doctrines of the Gospel*. Salt Lake City: Deseret News Press, 1945.

Robinson, Stephen E. *Believing Christ: The Parable of the Bicycle and Other Good News*. Salt Lake City: Deseret Book, 1992.

Smith, George Albert. *Sharing the Gospel with Others*. Salt Lake City: Deseret Book, 1948.

Smith, Joseph. *Teachings of the Prophet Joseph Smith*. Selected by Joseph Fielding Smith. Salt Lake City: Deseret Book, 1967.

Smith, Joseph F. *Gospel Doctrine*. Salt Lake City: Deseret Book, 1986.

Stackhouse, John G. *Evangelical Landscapes: Facing Critical Issues of the Day*. Grand Rapids: Baker Academic, 2002.

Stanley, Andy. *Am I Good Enough?* Sisters, Ore.: Multnomah, 2005.

———. *How Good Is Good Enough?* Sisters, Ore.: Multnomah, 2003.

Talmage, James E. *Jesus the Christ.* Salt Lake City: Deseret Book, 1983.

Warren, Rick. *The Purpose-Driven Life.* Grand Rapids, Mich.: Zondervan, 2002.

Whitney, Orson F. In Conference Report, Apr. 1929, 109–14.

Wirthlin, Joseph B. "Journey to Higher Ground." *Ensign*, Nov. 2005, 16–19.

Woodruff, Wilford. *Discourses of Wilford Woodruff.* Selected by G. Homer Durham. Salt Lake City: Bookcraft, 1946.

Yancey, Philip. *What's So Amazing about Grace?* Grand Rapids: Zondervan, 1997.

INDEX